The Collectio[n]
WEDDING MUSIC

Project Manager: Zobeida Pérez
Cover Illustration: Shigemi Shamada
Art Layout: Joe Klucar

CONTENTS

CLASSICAL MUSIC FOR THE WEDDING CEREMONY

POPULAR LOVE SONGS

MUSIC FOR THE RECEPTION

BRIDAL CHORUS
(Wedding March from "Lohengrin")

Music by
RICHARD WAGNER

Andantino

tranquillo
p
3
3

p
espressivo
cantando
p
pp

pp
pp
pp
p
dim.
pp
mf
smorz.
p
mf

AIR

(from the F Major Suite from "Water Music")

GEORGE FRIDERIC HANDEL
Arranged by PAMELA SCHULTZ

Adagio

mf - p

tr
mp

tr
f
tr

AVE MARIA

By FRANZ SCHUBERT

G11(♭9)
G7
Edim7
pray - er! We need Thy bless-ing this hour so
Fle - hen, aus die - sem Fel - sen starr und
ple - na, Ma - ri - a, gra - ti - a ple -
Fm
Fm6
E♭
F7
fair. Bless this love, this heav-en - ly hour so
wild soll mein Ge - bet su dir hin -
na, A - ve, A - ve! Do - mi -
E♭/B♭
B♭7
E♭
fair, bless this hour so fair! Safe
we - hen. Wir
nus, Do - mi - nus te cum. Bene -
E♭7
A♭/E♭
may we sleep be-neath Thy care, and
schla - fen si - cher bis zum Mor - gen, ob
dic - ta tu in mu - li - e - ri - bus, et

Eb7 Fm
guard this love we so ten-der-ly share! O
Men - schen noch _ so grau - sam sind. O
be - ne - dic - tus, et
Eb C7 Bbm
Maid - en, send your heav-en-ly an - swer! O
Jung - frau, sieh' der Jung - frau Sor - gen, o
be - ne - dic - tus fruc - tus ven - tris, ven - tris
fp
Bbm/Db Fdim7 Eb Eb7
Maid - en, hear _ this fer - vent pray'r.
Mut - ter, hör' _ ein bit - tend Kind!
tu - i Je - sus.
pp
Ab Fm6 Ab/Eb Eb7
A - ve Ma - ri -
A - ve Ma - ri -
A - ve Ma - ri -

A♭ A♭7 D♭/A♭ D♭dim/A♭ A♭
a!
a!
a!
Fm6 A♭/E♭ E♭7 Fm B♭m/D♭ E♭7
A - ve Ma - ri - a! O lis-ten to a
A - ve Ma - ri - a! Un - be -
A - ve Ma - ri - a! Ma - ter De -
A♭ A♭+ Fm/A♭
prayer! We pray, O Ma - ri - a, hear this
fleckt! Wenn wir auf diesen Fels hin -
i O - ra pro no - bis pec - ca -
G11(♭9) G7 Edim7
pray - er! We need Thy bless-ing this hour so
sin - ken zum Schlaf, und uns dein Schutz be -
to - ri - bus, O - ra, o - ra pro no -

Fm
Fm6
E♭/G
F7/C
fair.
Bless this love, this heav-en-ly hour so
deckt, wird weich der har - te Fels uns
bis, O - ra, o - ra pro no -
E♭/B♭
B♭7
E♭
fair, bless this hour so fair! Safe
dün - ken. Du
bis pec - ca - to - ri - bus, nunc,
E♭7
A♭/E♭
may we sleep be-neath Thy care, and
la - chelst, Ro - sen-duf - te we - hen in
et in ho - ra mor - tis, in
E♭7
Fm
guard this love we so ten-der-ly share! O
die - ser dump - fen Fel - sen-kluft; o
ho - ra mor - tis no - strae, in

E♭ C7 B♭m
pp
Maid - en, send your heav-en - ly an - swer! O
Mut - ter, hör' des Kin - des Fle - hen, o
ho - ra mor - tis, mor - tis no - strae, in
fp
B♭m/D♭ Fdim7 E♭ E♭7
Maid - en, hear this fer - vent prayer!
Jung - frau, ei - ne Jung - frau ruft!
ho - ra mor - tis no - strae
pp
A♭ Fm6 A♭/E♭ E♭7
A - ve Ma - ri -
A - ve Ma - ri -
A - ve Ma - ri -
A♭ A♭7 D♭/A♭ D♭dim/A♭ A♭
a!
a!
a!

Fm6 Ab/Eb Eb7
A - ve Ma - ri -
A - ve Ma - ri -
A - ve Ma - ri -
mf
Fm Bbm/Db Eb7
a! O lis - ten to a
a! Rei - ne
a! gra - ti - a ple -
Ab Ab+ Fm/Ab
prayer! O give to this love e - ter - nal
Magd! Der Er - de und der Luft Dä -
na, Ma - ri - a, gra - ti - a
G11(b9) G7 Edim7
wis - dom, and keep it safe from harm and
mo - nen, von dei - nes Au - ges Huld ver -
ple - na, Ma - ri - a, gra - ti - a ple -

Fm
Fm6
E♭/G
F7/C
woe.
Make this love a love that will con-stant-ly
jagt,
sie kön - nen. hier nicht bei uns
na.
A - ve, A - ve! Do - mi -
E♭/B♭
B♭7
E♭
grow, safe from harm and woe.
O
woh - nen!
Wir
nus, Do - mi - nus te cum;
Be - ne -
E♭7
A♭/E♭
Maid - en guard our love from harm,
O
woll'n uns still dem Schick - sal beu - gen,
da
dic - ta tu in mu - li - e - ri - bus,
et
E♭7
Fm
Maid - en, guard our love from harm.
O
uns dein heil' - ger Trost an - weht;
du
be - ne - dic - tus,
et

E♭
C7
B♭m
Maid - en, send thy heav-en - ly an - swer, O
Jung - frau wol - le hold dich nei - gen dem
be - ne - dic - tus fruc - tus ven - tris, ven - tris
fp
B♭m/D♭
Fdim
E♭
E♭7
bless this love from your throne - a - bove!
Kind, das für den Va - ter fleht!
tu - i, Je - sus.
pp
A♭
Fm6
A♭/E♭
E♭7
A♭
A♭7
A - ve Ma - ri - a!
A - ve Ma - ri - a!
A - ve Ma - ri - a!
pp
D♭/A♭
D♭dim/A♭
A♭
dim.
pp

HORNPIPE

(from the D Major Suite from "Water Music")

GEORGE FRIDERIC HANDEL
Arranged by PAMELA SCHULTZ

mp

f
p

f

tr

mf
p

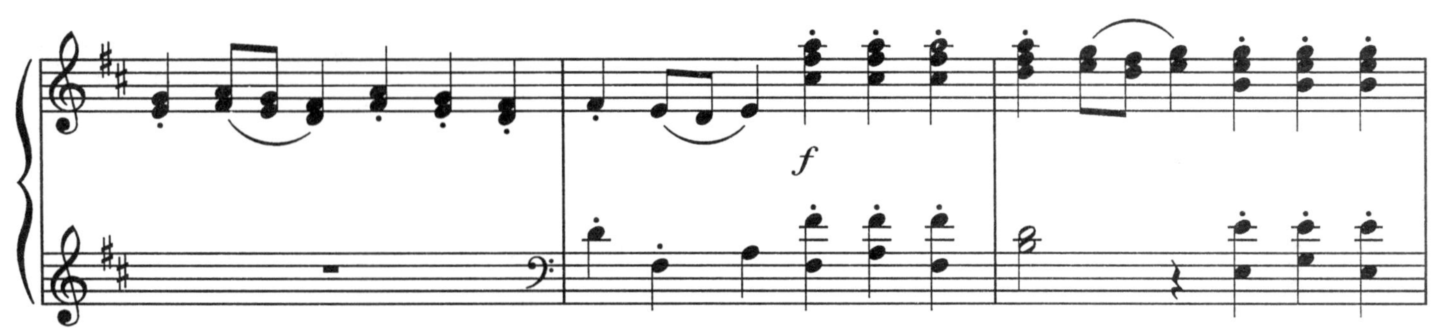
f

tr
ff

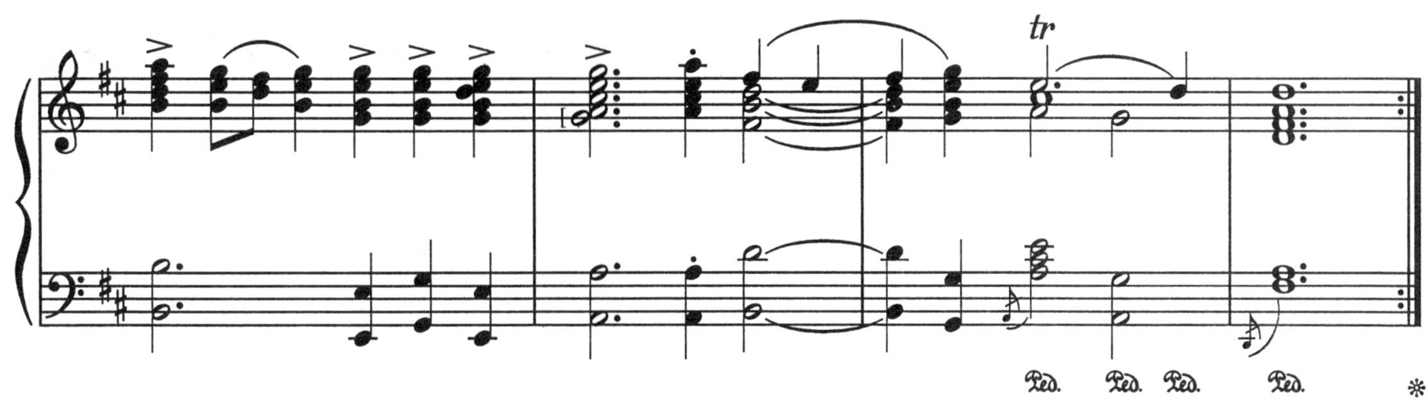
tr

AVE MARIA

(From the First Prelude of Johann Sebastian Bach)

Adapted by CHARLES GOUNOD

Do - mi-nus te - cum, be - ne -
God is with thee. Bless - ed,
cresc.
pp
cresc.
dic - ta tu in mu - li -
bless - ed art thou, art thou a-bove all
dim.
pp
cresc.
e - ri-bus et be - ne - dic - tus
wo - men, Bless - ed be thine off - spring,
p
cresc.
p
fruc - tus - ven - tris
Bless - ed be thy son, the son of
cresc.

tu - i Je - sus. Sanc - ta Ma-
God, the Lord most high! Bless - ed Ma-
dim.
p
ri - a, sanc - ta Ma - ri - a, Ma-
ri - a! Bless - ed Ma - ri - a! Ma-
cresc. molto
f
ri - a, o - ra pro - no - bis,
ri - a! Pray, oh, pray for us,
p
pp
cresc. molto
no - bis pec - ca - to - ri - bus,
for us wretch - ed sin - ners,

f
nunc et in ho - ra, in
Now and when the hour of our
f
ff
ho - ra mor - tis nos - trae,
death our death o'er takes us,
(,)
A - men!
A - men!
dim.
p
A - men!
A - men!
pp
poco rit.
Ped.
*

CANON IN D
(Pachelbel)

JOHANN PACHELBEL
Arranged by ROBERT SCHULTZ

mf
pp
mp
p

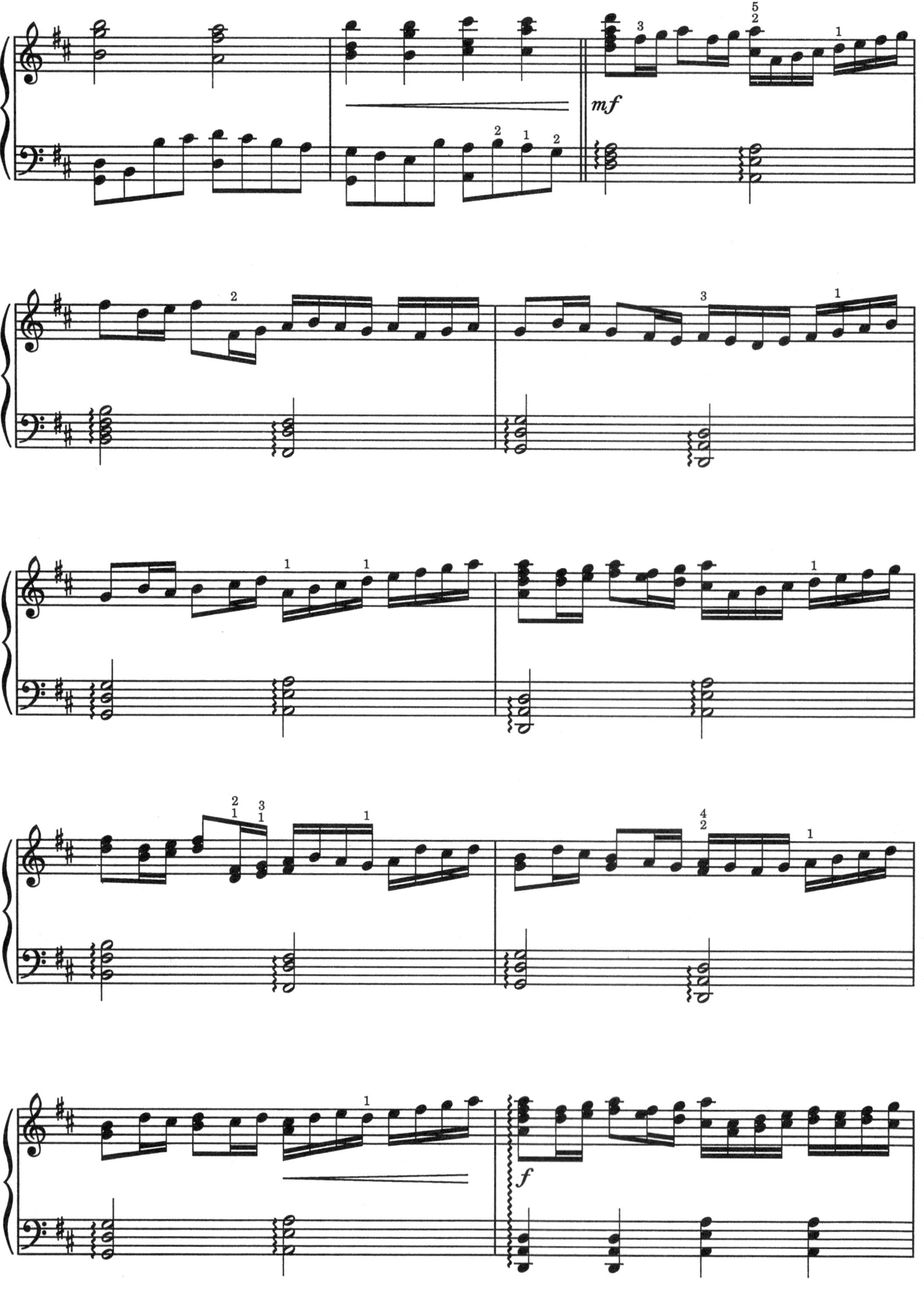

mf
f

2
1
3
1
3
1
5
3
3
1
mf
2
1
mp
4
1
3
1
2
3
1
p
espressivo
pp

mp

cresc.
mf
Ped.
Ped.
pedal simile
2
3
3
4

4
3
4
f
dim. poco a poco

espressivo
p
(poco staccato)
mp
mf

f
ff
l.h.

TRUMPET VOLUNTARY

HENRY PURCELL
Arranged by PAMELA SCHULTZ

tr
p
tr
tr
mf
tr
tr
f

tr
tr
mf
ff
D.C. al Fine

JESU, JOY OF MAN'S DESIRING

JOHANN SEBASTIAN BACH

3
3
3

3
3

3
3

rit.

THE WEDDING MARCH
(From "A Midsummer Night's Dream")

Music by
FELIX MENDELSSOHN

Allegro

2.
3
3
ff
sf
ff
1.
2.

AFTER ALL
(Love Theme from "Chances Are")

Words and Music by
DEAN PITCHFORD
and TOM SNOW

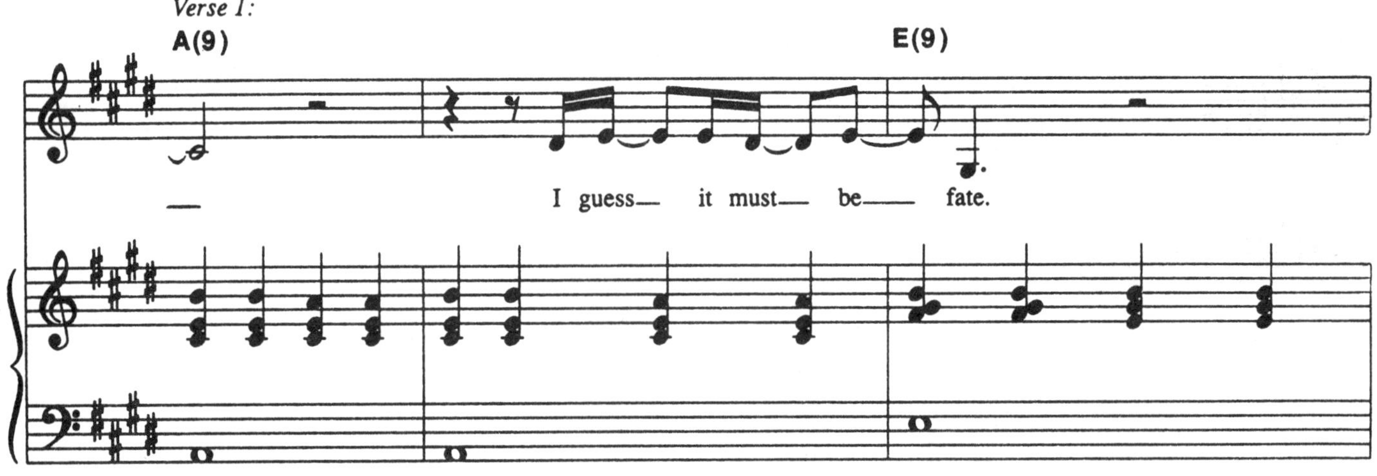

B
She:
E/G♯
A(9)
straight.
I still re-mem - ber when

C♯m7
F♯m
E/G♯
your kiss was so brand new.
Ev-ery mem-o-ry re-peats, ev-ery

A
E/G♯
Both:
A
B
A/B B
step I take re-treats. Ev-ery jour-ney al - ways brings me back to you. Af-ter
cresc.

Chorus:
E
C♯m
all the stops and starts, we keep com-in' back to these two hearts, two
f

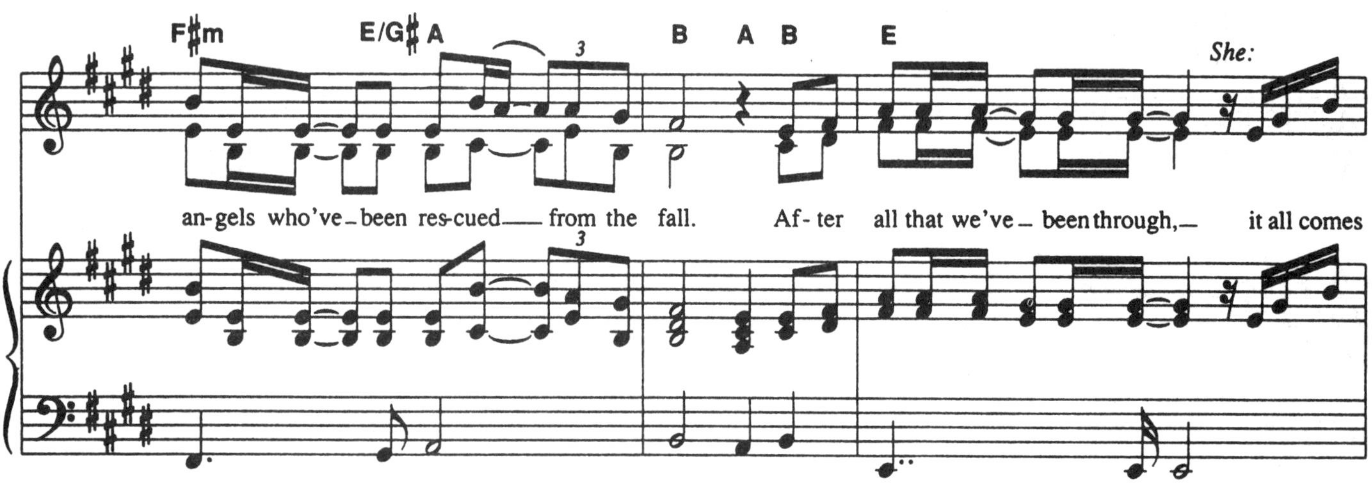
F♯m
E/G♯
A
B
A
B
E
She:
an-gels who've been res-cued from the fall. Af-ter all that we've been through, it all comes

G♯m7
G♯/B♯
C♯m
Both:
A
He:
down to me and you. I guess it's meant to be, for

To Coda
1.
To next strain
Bsus
B
E
A/E
E
ev - er you and me,
af - ter all.
2. When love is tru - ly
dim.

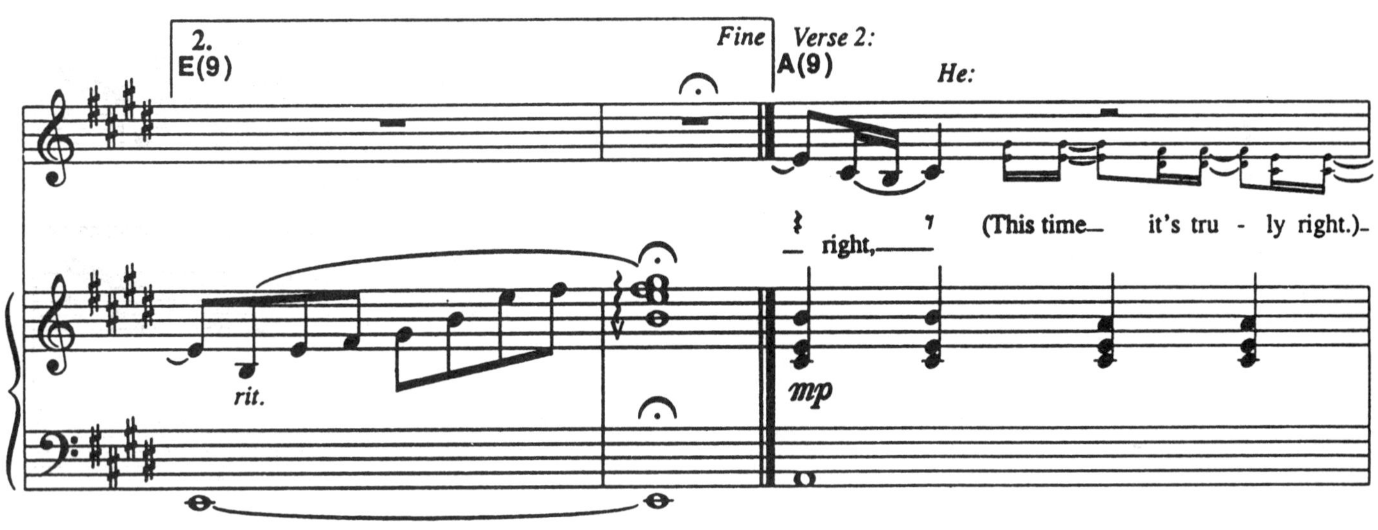
2.
Fine
Verse 2:
E(9)
A(9)
He:
right,
(This time it's tru - ly right.)
rit.
mp

She:
E(9)
C♯m7
Both:
E/G♯
A
it lives from year to year.
It chang - es as it

D.S. al Coda
B
She:
E/G♯
A(9)
Both:
B
A/B B
goes, oh, and on the way it grows,— but it nev- er dis- ap- pears.— Af- ter
cresc.

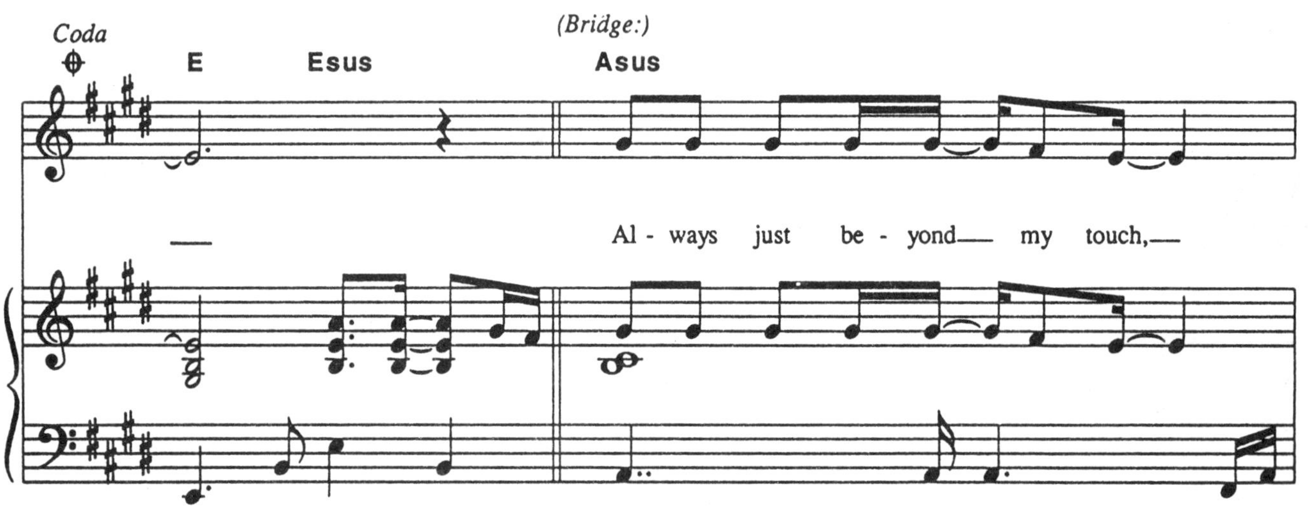
Coda
E
Esus
(Bridge:)
Asus
— Al - ways just be - yond— my touch,—

D.S. al Fine
G♯/B♯
C♯m
A B
You know I need- ed you— so much. Af- ter all, what else is liv- in' for?— Af- ter

ALL I EVER NEED IS YOU

Words and Music by
JIMMY HOLIDAY and
EDDIE REEVES

C
G
Em
A7
Am7
D7
G
And lov - ing you is all I ask, Hon - ey, All I Ev - er Need_ Is You.
C
D
C
Win - ters come and they go, and we watch_ the melt - ing
Bm
C
G
Bm
Em
G
snow._ Sure as sum - mer fol - lows spring, all the things_ you do
C
Am7
Am7
(D Bass)
D7
G
give me a rea - son to build my world a - round you. Some men fol - low rain - bows, I am
rit.
a tempo

B7 Em G7

told, Some men search for sil - ver some_ for gold.

C G Em A7

I have found my treas - ure in your soul, Hon - ey, All I Ev - er Need_ Is

D7 G B7

You. With - out love I'd nev - er find_ the way, Through

Em G7 C

ups and downs of ev - 'ry sin - gle day. I won't sleep at night_ un - til you

G Em A7 Am7 D7 G C G

say, my Hon - ey, All I Ev - er Need_ Is You.

ALL MY LOVE

Words and Music by
AL JOLSON, SAUL CHAPLIN
and HARRY AKST

A7 Dm D7 Gm 3fr. Dm
with you. As the years un - fold they can on - ly bring Just the
mf più mosso
A7 Dm D7 Gm 3fr.
con - stant joy of an end - less spring. And our dreams un - told, that were
Dm A E7 A A7 Tempo I Dm
so i - deal Will all fade as we make them real. I prom -
rit.
mp
A7 Dm D D7 Gm 3fr. A A7
ise this, by the stars a - bove: Dear, that I'll spend
Dm Gm 3fr. Bb7 Dm A7 Dm A7 Dm
1. 2.
all my life giv - ing you ALL MY LOVE. LOVE.

ALL THE WAY

Lyric by
SAMMY CAHN

Music by
JAMES VAN HEUSEN

G7
1.
Cm
Bbm7
Eb7-5
Ab
3fr.
4fr.
That's how it's got to feel;
on - ly a fool would
Deep - er than the
Bb7
Bo7
Cm
Cm7
F7
Fm7-5
Bb7
deep blue sea is, that's how deep it goes, if it's real.
3
Cm
Abm6
Eb
Db9
C7
Am7-5
Bb9
2.
say, But if you let me love you, it's for sure I'm gon-na love you ALL THE
Gm7-5
C7
Fm7-5
Bb7-5
Eb
Db9
Eb6/9
WAY, ALL THE WAY.
rall.
8vb

ALWAYS

Moderately slow ♩ = 66

G(9) D/G Dm/G C

mf

Am7 /D G(9)

Boy:

G D/G Dm/G C Am7 /D G(9)

1. Girl, you are to me all that a woman should be, and I dedicate my life to you always.
2. Come with me, my sweet; let's go make a family. And they will bring us joy for always.

mp

Girl:

G D/G Dm/G C

A love like yours is rare; it must have been sent from up above. And I
Oh, boy, I love you so; I can't find enough ways to let you know. But you

Always - 3 - 1

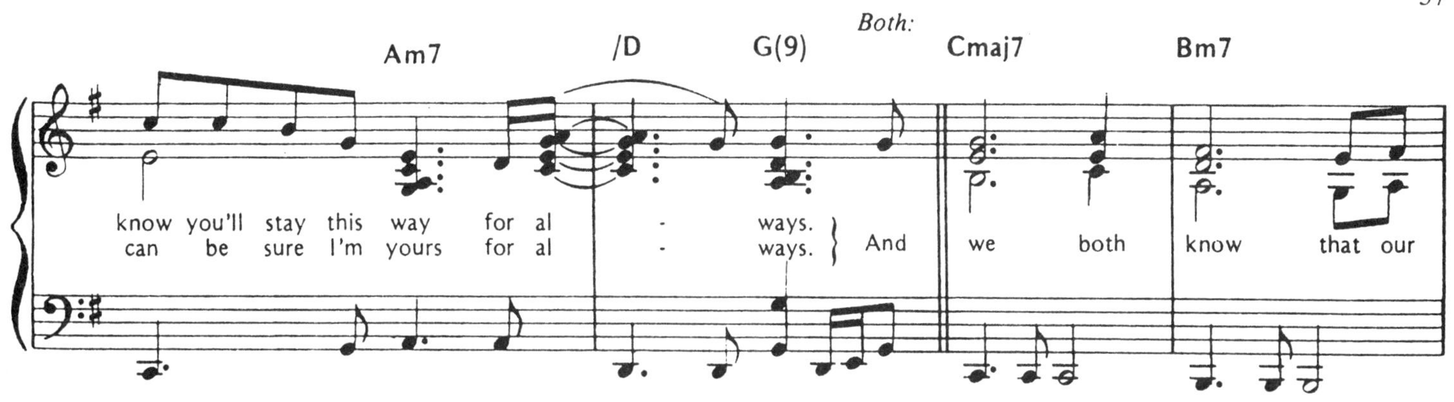
Both:
Am7 /D G(9) Cmaj7 Bm7
know you'll stay this way for al - ways.
can be sure I'm yours for al - ways.
And we both know that our

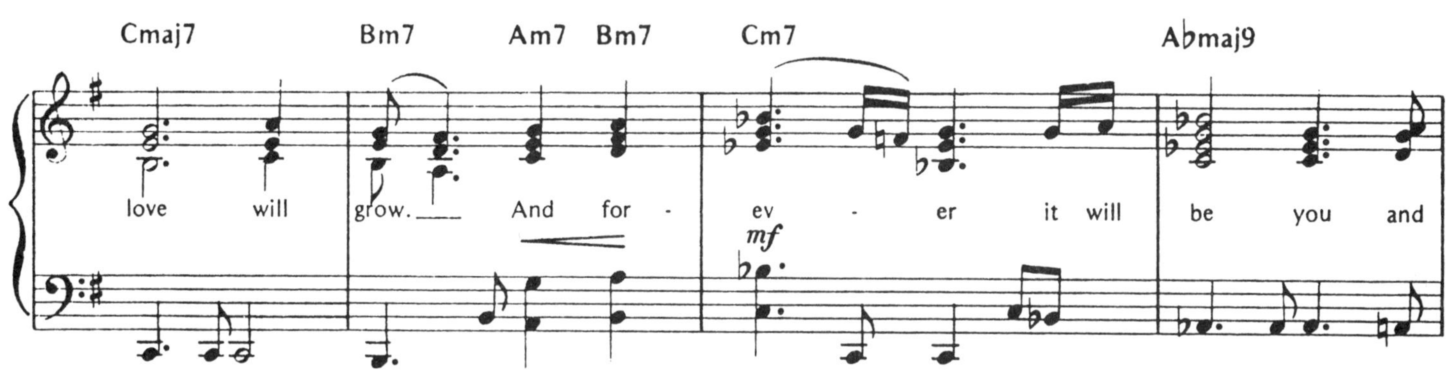
Cmaj7 Bm7 Am7 Bm7 Cm7 A♭maj9
love will grow. And for - ev - er it will be you and
mf

Chorus:
Am7/D D C/E D/F♯ G D/G Dm/G C
me.
Ooh, you're like the sun, chas - ing all the rain a - way.
f

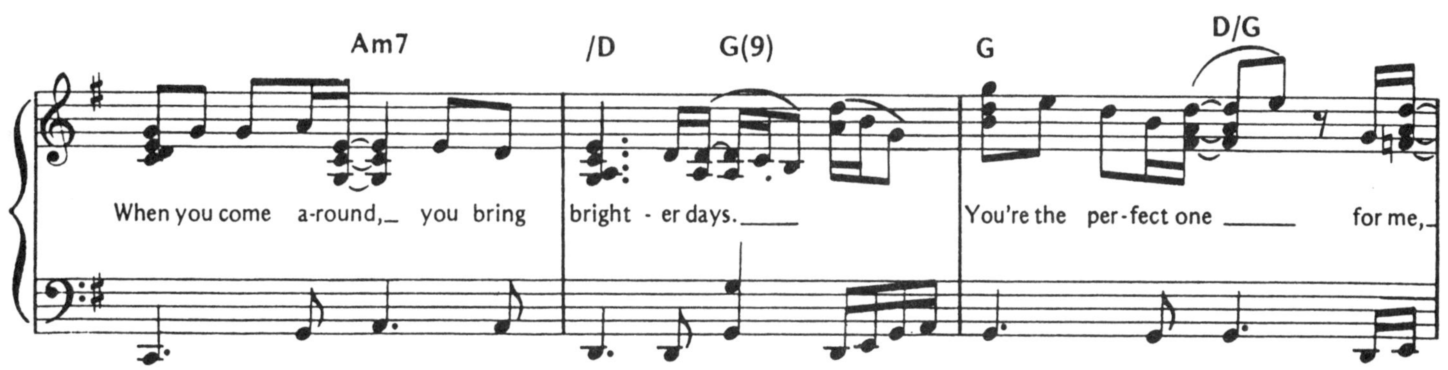
Am7 /D G(9) G D/G
When you come a-round, you bring bright - er days.
You're the per-fect one for me,

1.
D.S. 𝄋
Dm/G
C
Am7
/D
G(9)
and you for-ev-er will be. And
I will love you so for
al - ways.

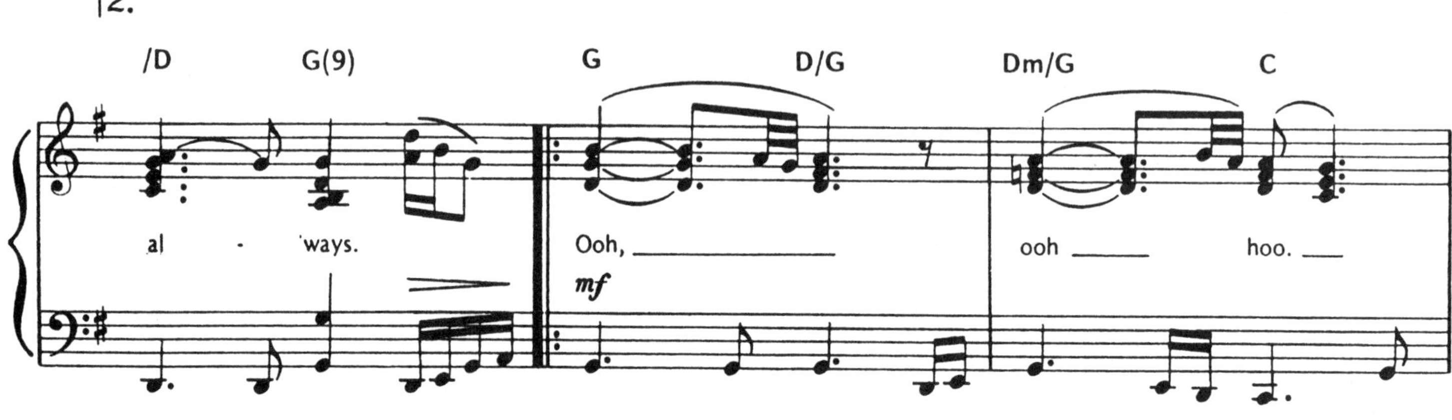
2.
/D
G(9)
G
D/G
Dm/G
C
al - 'ways.
Ooh,
mf
ooh
hoo.

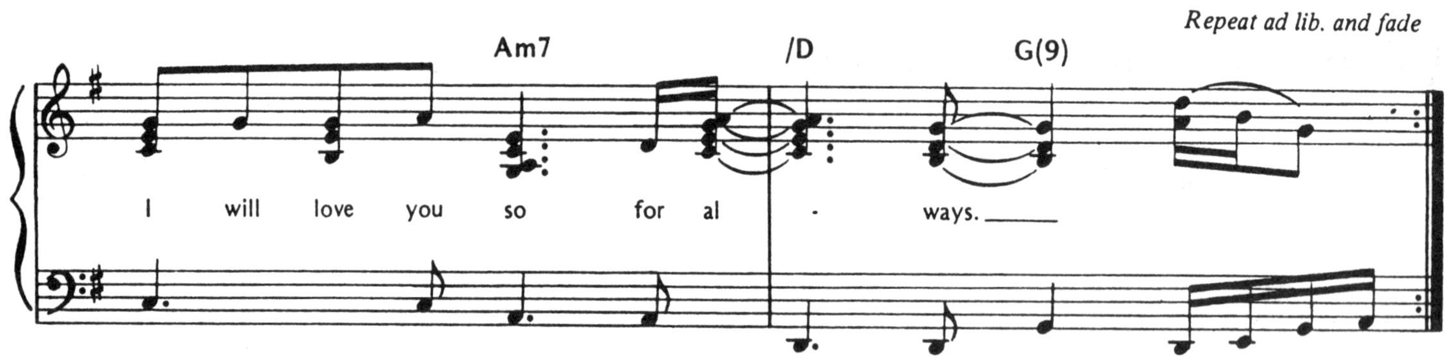
Repeat ad lib. and fade
Am7
/D
G(9)
I will love you so for al - ways.

BUTTERFLY KISSES

Words and Music by
BOB CARLISLE and RANDY THOMAS

C
Dm7
C/E
Fsus2 sus4
Gsus
G
dad-dy's lit - tle girl. As I drop to my knees by her bed at night,
give her a - way. Stand-ing in the bride room just star-ing at her, she
Dm7
C/E
Fsus2 sus4
Gsus
G
F(9)/A
G/B
she talks to Je - sus, and I close my eyes. And I thank God for all of the
asks me what I'm think - ing, and I say, "I'm not sure. I just feel like I'm los - ing my
C
F(9)/A
F/G
joy in my life, oh, but most of all, for
ba - by girl." Then she leaned o - ver and gave me
Chorus 1 & 3:
Csus2 sus4
C
Csus2 sus4
C
but - ter - fly kiss - es af - ter bed - time prayer, stick - in'
but - ter - fly kiss - es with her ma - ma there, stick - in'
mf

Csus2 sus4
C
G/C
Asus2 sus4
Am
G
lit - tle white flow - ers all up in her hair.
lit - tle white flow - ers all up in her hair.
F(9)
C/E
"Walk be - side the po - ny, dad - dy, it's my first ride." "I
"Walk me down the aisle, dad - dy, it's just a - bout time." "Does my
F(9)
C/E
know the cake looks fun - ny, dad - dy, but I sure tried." Oh, with
wed - ding gown look pret - ty, dad - dy?" "Dad - dy, don't cry." Oh, with
F/A
G/B
C
Dsus
D
To Coda
all that I've done wrong, I must have done some-thing right to de-serve a
all that I've done wrong, I must have done some-thing right to de-serve her

F(9)
G7sus
Csus2 sus4
C
C(9)
hug ev-'ry morn - ing and but-ter-fly kiss - es at night.
mp
p
Verse 2:
Am7
C
Am7
2. Sweet six - teen to - day; she's look - ing like her ma - ma a lit - tle
mp
3
C
Dm7
C/E
F6 9
Gsus
G
more ev - 'ry day. One part wom - an, the oth - er part girl; to
Dm7
C/E
F(9)
G7sus
G
F(9)/A
G/B
per-fume and make - up from rib-bons and curls; try - ing her wings out in a

C(9)
F(9)/A
Gsus
great big world. But I re - mem - ber
Chorus 2:
Csus2 sus4
C
Csus2 sus4
C
Csus2 sus4
C
but-ter-fly kiss-es af-ter bed-time prayer, stick-in' lit-tle white flow - ers all
mf
G/C
Asus2 sus4
Am
G
F(9)
up in her hair. "You know how much I love you, dad - dy, but if
C/E
F(9)
C/E
you don't mind, I'm on-ly gon-na kiss you on the cheek this time." Oh, with

F/A
G/B
C
Dsus
D
all that I've done wrong, I must have done some-thing right to de-serve her
F(9)
G7sus
Csus2 sus4
C
Csus2 sus4
C
love ev-'ry morn-ing and but-ter-fly kiss-es at night.
(All the pre-cious
cresc.
Bridge:
E♭
Dm
Csus2 sus4
C
Csus2 sus4
C
time.)
Oh, like the wind, the years go by.
(Pre-cious but-ter-
f
E♭
Dm7
F/A
G
D.S. 𝄋 al Coda
fly, spread your wings and fly.)
dim.

Coda

F(9) G7sus F(9)/A

love ev-'ry morn - ing and but-ter-fly kiss - es.__ I could-n't ask God_ for more,_ man,

G/B A♭maj 9 C/G

poco rit.

this is what love is.___ I know I've got__ to let__ her go, but I'll al - ways____ re-mem - ber__

freely

poco rit.

F(9) G7sus

ev-'ry hug in the morn - ing and but-ter-fly kiss - es.________

freely

a tempo

C sus2 sus4 C G/A G7sus C(9)

a tempo

rit. e dim.

mp

AMAZED

Words and Music by
MARV GREEN, AIMEE MAYO
and CHRIS LINDSEY

Am7 (A♭m7) — F (F♭)

I can hear your thoughts, I can see your dreams.

Chorus:

D (D♭) — A (A♭)

I don't know how you do what you do. I'm so in love with you.

Bm (B♭m) — G (G♭)

It just keeps get-ting bet-ter.

D (D♭) — A (A♭)

I wan-na spend the rest of my life with you by my side

Bm (B♭m) — D/A (D♭/A♭) — G (G♭)

for-ev-er and ev-er.

F
F♭
G
G♭
Ev - 'ry lit - tle thing that you do,
ba - by, I'm a - mazed by you.
1.
A
A♭
2.
A
A♭
C
C♭
D
D♭
A
A♭
C
C♭
G
G♭
Chorus:
Dsus
D
D♭sus
D♭
N.C.
G
G♭
A
A♭
Ev - 'ry lit - tle thing that you do,
I'm so in love with you.
Bm
B♭m
D/A
D♭/A♭
G
G♭
It just keeps get - ting bet - ter.

Verse 2:
The smell of your skin,
The taste of your kiss,
The way you whisper in the dark.
Your hair all around me,
Baby, you surround me;
You touch every place in my heart.
Oh, it feels like the first time every time.
I wanna spend the whole night in your eyes.
(To Chorus:)

ANGEL OF MINE

Words and Music by
RHETT LAWRENCE and
TRAVON POTTS

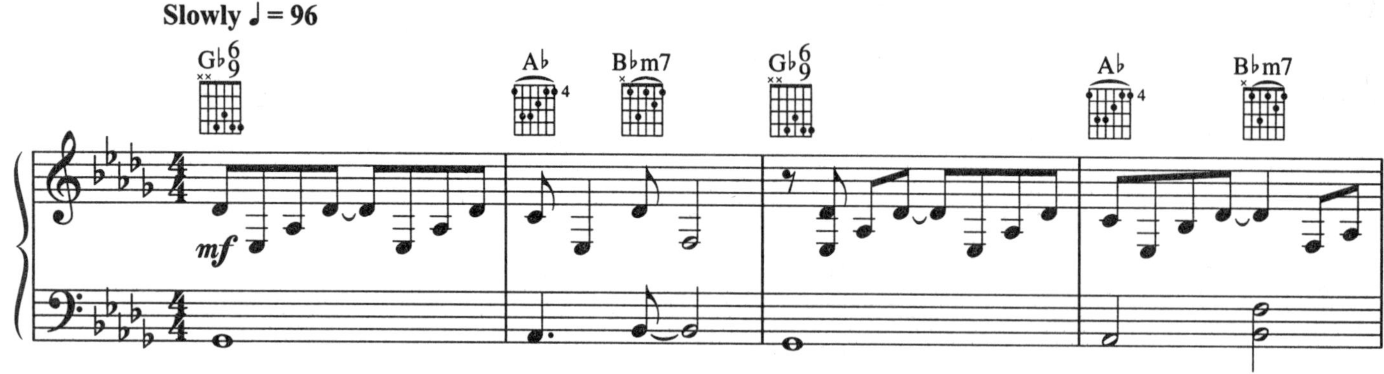

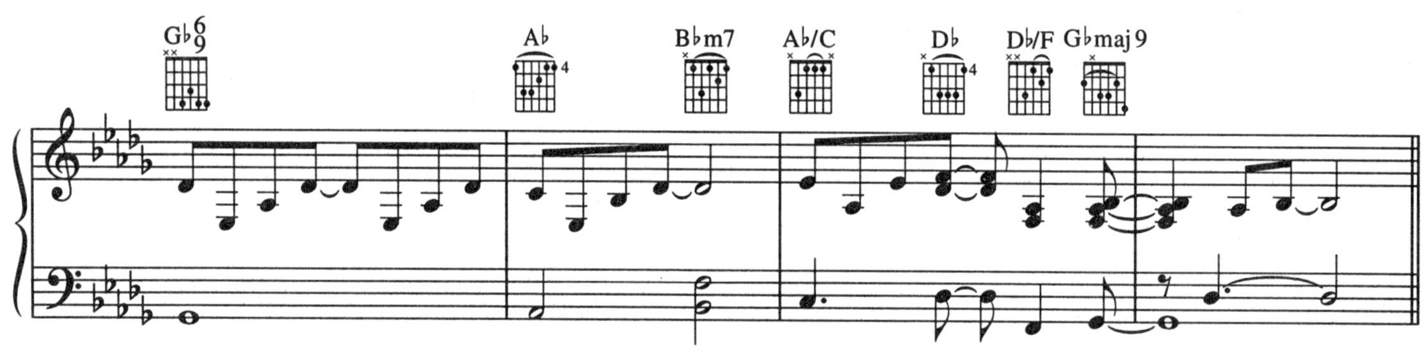

A♭
B♭m7
G♭6/9
in - side of you.
Some - thing I thought that I would
A♭
B♭m7
A♭/C
D♭
D♭/F
G♭maj9
nev - er find, an - gel of mine.
Verses 2 & 3:
G♭6/9
A♭
B♭m7
2. I look at you look - ing at me
3. Noth - ing means more to me than what we share.
G♭6/9
A♭
B♭m7
G♭6/9
Now I know why they say the best things are free.
No one in this whole world can ev - er com - pare.
I'm gon - na love you, boy, you
Last night, the way you moved is

A♭
B♭m7
A♭/C
D♭
D♭/F
G♭maj 9
are so fine, an - gel of mine.
still on my mind, an - gel of mine.
Pre-chorus 1 & 2:
E♭m7
F 7(♯5)
G♭(9)
1. How you changed my world, you'll nev - er know. I'm dif - f'rent now, you
2. What you mean to me, you'll nev - er know. Deep in - side I
Chorus:
C♭
G♭6/9
A♭
B♭m7
helped me grow.
need to show.
You came in - to my life straight from a - bove.
G♭6/9
A♭
B♭m7
G♭6/9
When I lost all hope, you showed me love. I'm check - ing for you, boy, you're

To Coda
1.
A♭
B♭m7
A♭/C
D♭
D♭/F
G♭maj9
right on time,
an - gel of mine.
2.
Bridge:
A♭7sus
A♭
I nev - er knew I could feel each mo - ment
F7/A
F7(♭9)
B♭m7
G♭9
as if it were new.
Ev - 'ry breath that I take, the love
A♭/C
F7
B♭m7
A♭/C
D♭
B♭7
A♭7/C
B♭7/D
that we make,
I on - ly share it with you,
you, you, you.

Verse 4:
G♭6/9
A♭
B♭m7
G♭6/9
4. When I first saw you, I al - read - y knew___ there was some-thing
A♭
B♭m7
G♭6/9
A♭
B♭m7
in - side___ of you. Some-thing I thought that I would nev - er find,___
A♭/C
D♭
D♭/F
G♭maj 9
D.S.𝄋 al Coda
an - gel_____ of mine._____ You
Coda
Pre-chorus 3:
E♭m7
F 7(♯5)
3. How you changed my world, you'll nev - er know.___

G♭(9) C♭

I'm dif - f'rent now, you helped me grow.

Verse 5:

G♭6/9 A♭ B♭m7 G♭6/9

5. I look at you look - ing at me. Now I know why they say the

A♭ B♭m7 G♭6/9

best things are free. I'm check - ing for you, boy, you're

A♭ B♭m7 A♭/C D♭ D♭/F G♭maj9

right on time, an - gel of mine.

rit.

BE MY BABY

Words and Music by
ELLIE GREENWICH, JEFF BARRY and PHIL SPECTOR

G♯7
C♯7
So won't you say you love me? I'll make you so proud of me.
Oh, since the day I saw you, I have been wait - ing for you.
F♯7
B
We'll make 'em turn their heads ev - 'ry place we go.
You know I will a - dore you till e - ter - ni - ty.
So won't you please
Chorus:
E
C♯m
be my lit - tle ba - by?
(Be my, be my ba - by,) (my one and
A
Say you'll be my dar - lin'.
Be my ba - by
on - ly ba - by.) (Be my, be my ba - by,)

1.
2.
B7
now,
(my one and
woh, oh, oh, oh.
on - ly ba - by.)
woh, oh, oh, oh,
on - ly ba - by.)
E
F♯m7
B
oh.
E
F♯m7
B
So come on and
E
C♯m
please
(Be my, be my ba - by,)
Be my lit-tle ba - by.
(my one and

A
Say you'll be my dar - lin'.
on - ly ba - by.)
(Be my, be my ba - by,)
Be my ba - by
B7
N.C.
now,
woh, oh, oh, oh.
(my one and on - ly ba - by.)
Perc.:
E
C♯m
(oh.)
Be my lit-tle ba - by,
oh,
(Be my, be my ba - by,)
(my one and on - ly ba - by.)
A
B7
Repeat ad lib. and fade
oh,
woh, oh, oh, oh.
(Be my, be my ba - by,)
(my one and on - ly ba - by.)

COULD I HAVE THIS DANCE

Words and Music by
WAYLAND HOLYFIELD and BOB HOUSE

Moderately Slow

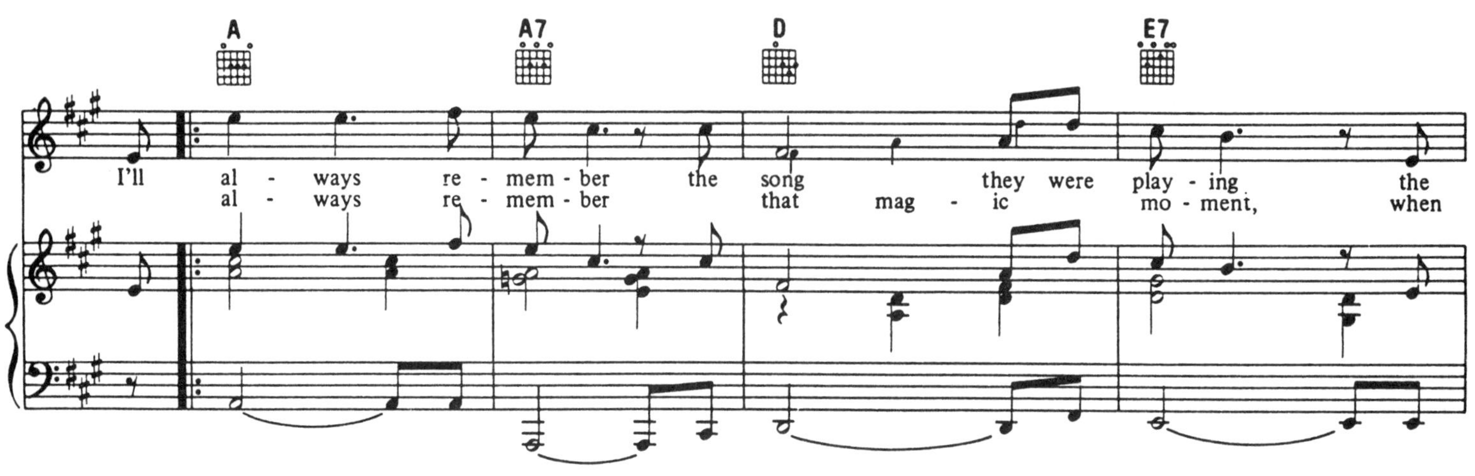

A
A7
D
E7
swayed to the mu - sic ___ and held to each oth - er, ___
we moved to - geth - er, ___ I knew for - ev - er ___
D
E7
A
E
Bm/F♯
E7/G♯
I fell in love with ___ you.
you're all I'll ev - er ___ need.
Could
A
A7
D
I have this dance for the rest of my life? Would
mf
E7
D
E7
you be my part - ner ___ ev - 'ry night?

A
A7
D
Dm
When we're to - geth - er, it feels so right. Could
A
E7
To Coda
1
A
Bm7/E
I have this dance for the rest of my life? 2. I'll
mp
2
A
E
Bm/F♯
E7/G♯
D.S. al Coda
life? Could
3
CODA
E7
rest of my
A
Bm7
E7
A
life?
f

ENDLESS LOVE

Words and Music by
LIONEL RICHIE

B♭
F/A
E♭
step I make.
sist your charms.
And I,
And love,
mf
E♭/F
F
B♭
F/A
Gm
Dm/F
3
I want to share all my love
I'll be a fool for you I'm
E♭
E♭/F
F
B♭
with you,
sure;
no one else will do.
you know I don't mind.
B♭9
E♭
E♭/F
F
And your eyes,
'Cause you,
they tell me how
you mean the

B♭
F/A
Gm
F6
E♭
much you care.
world to me.
Oh, yes, you will
Oh, I know
Dm7
Cm7
E♭/F
B♭
al - ways be my end-less love.
I've found in you my end-less
8va
mp
B♭
love.
mp
E♭
E♭/F
Fsus
F
B♭

Eb
Eb/F
Bb
Eb
Oh, and love.
cresc.
mf
Eb/F
F
Bb
F/A
Gm7
F/A
Eb
I'll be that fool for you I'm sure;
Eb/F
F
Eb
Bb9
Eb
you know I don't mind.
And yes,

Eb/F
F
Bb
F/A
Gm
Dm/F
Ebmaj7
you'll be the on - ly one.
No one can de-ny
Dm7
Ebmaj7
Dm7
Ebmaj7
this love I have in - side.
I'll give it all to
Dm7
Cm7
Eb/F
Bb
you my love, my love, my end - less love.
Eb
E/F
Fsus
F
Eb/Bb
Bb
rit.

EVERGREEN

Love Theme from "A Star Is Born"

Words by
PAUL WILLIAMS

Music by
BARBRA STREISAND

Bm/A
A
A/G♯
love, fresh as the morn - ing air.
F♯m
C♯m7
4 fr.
One love that is shared by two,
Bm7
G
I have found with you.
E
E7sus4
E7
A
D/E
Like a rose un - der the A - pril snow,

Bm7
D/E
I was al - ways cer - tain
A
A/G♯
F♯m
love would grow.
Love,
C♯m7
4 fr.
3
age - less and ev - er - green,
3
Dmaj7
Cmaj7
G/A
3 fr.
A7
sel - dom seen by two.
cresc.

Dmaj7
D6
C♯m7
4 fr.
You and I will make each night a first,
mf
Dmaj7
E/D
C♯m7
G/A
A7
3 fr.
ev-'ry day a be-gin-ning.
8va
Dmaj7
G♯7sus4
G♯7
C♯m7
C
Spir-its rise and their dance is un-re-hearsed.
loco
A/B
B7
D/E
They warm and ex-cite us 'cause we have the bright-est
cresc. e allarg.

Amaj7
Gmaj7/A
love,
two lights that shine as
Bm7
D/E
one,
morn - ing glo - ry and the
A
A/G♯
F♯m
mid-night sun.
Time, we've learned to
C♯m7
4 fr.
G/A
3 fr.
sail a - bove;
time won't change the

Dmaj7
Dm(maj7)
A
meaning of
one love,
ageless and
B/A
Bb/A
ever
ever
A
Bb/A
B/A
C/A
3 fr.
green.
B/A
Bb/A
A
rit. e dim.
mp

(EVERYTHING I DO) I DO IT FOR YOU

Written by
BRYAN ADAMS, ROBERT JOHN LANGE
and MICHAEL KAMEN

Ebm
Db/F
Ebm/Gb
Db/F
Ebm
Db/F
tell me it's not worth try - in' for. You can't tell me it's not worth dy - in'
Ebm/Gb
Db/Ab
Ab5
for. You know it's true, ev-ery-thing I do, I do it for
Db2
Verse:
Db
you.
cresc.
mf
2. Look in-to your heart,
Ab/Db
Gb
Absus
Ab5
you will find there's noth - ing there to hide. Take me as I
Db
Ab/Db
Gb
am, take my life. I would give it all, I would

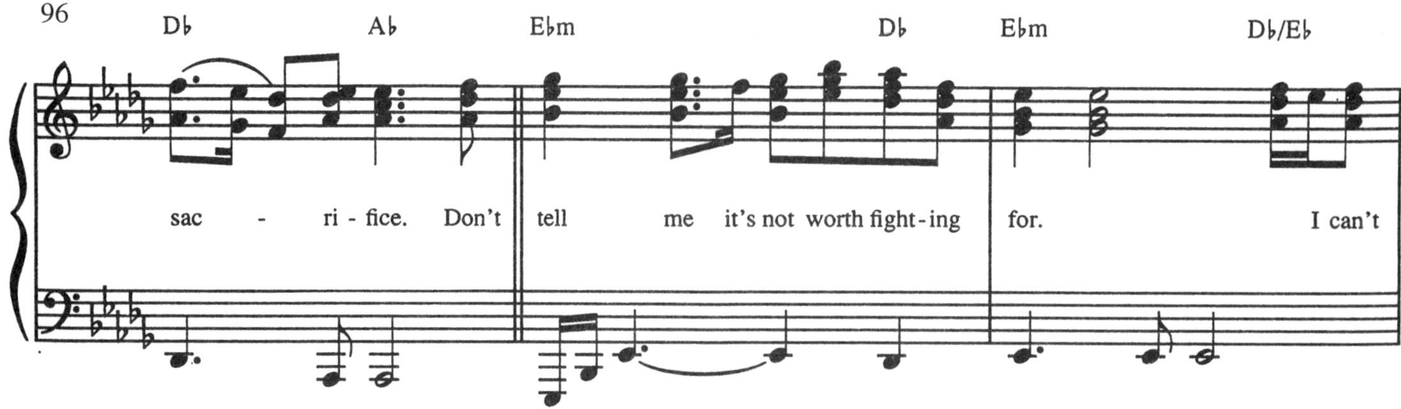
D♭ A♭ E♭m D♭ E♭m D♭/E♭
sac - ri - fice. Don't tell me it's not worth fight - ing for. I can't

E♭m D♭ E♭m D♭
help it, there's noth-ing I want more. You know it's true, ev-ery-thing I

A♭5 D♭ D♭sus D♭
do, I do it for you. There's
cresc.

C♭ F♭ C♭
no love like your love, and no oth - er could give
f

G♭
D♭
A♭
more love. There's
no - where un-less
you're there, all the

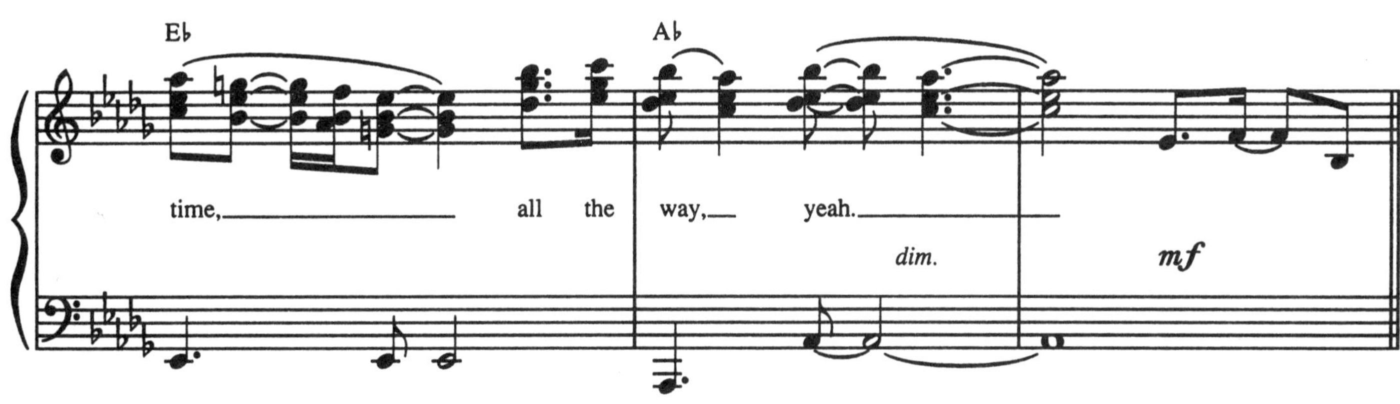
E♭
A♭
time, all the
way, yeah.
dim.
mf

G♭
D♭
D♭sus
(instrumental solo . . .

1.
2.
D♭
D♭
E♭m
Oh, you can't
tell me it's not worth try - in'
. . . end solo)

A♭
E♭m
A♭
G♭/A♭
for.
I can't
help
it,
there's noth-ing
I
want
more.
Yeah, I would
cresc.
f

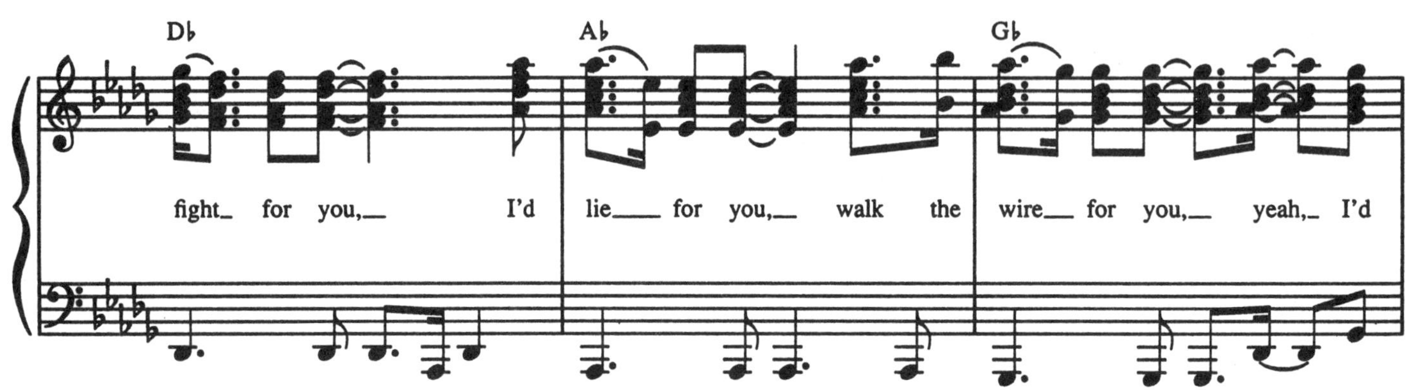
D♭
A♭
G♭
fight for you,
I'd
lie for you,
walk the
wire for you,
yeah, I'd

G♭m
D♭/A♭
die for you.
You know it's
true,
ev-ery-thing I
dim.
mp

A♭sus
A♭
G♭
G♭6
D♭
do,
oh,
I do it for
you.
rit.
dim.
p

FLYING WITHOUT WINGS

Words and Music by
WAYNE HECTOR
and STEVE MAC

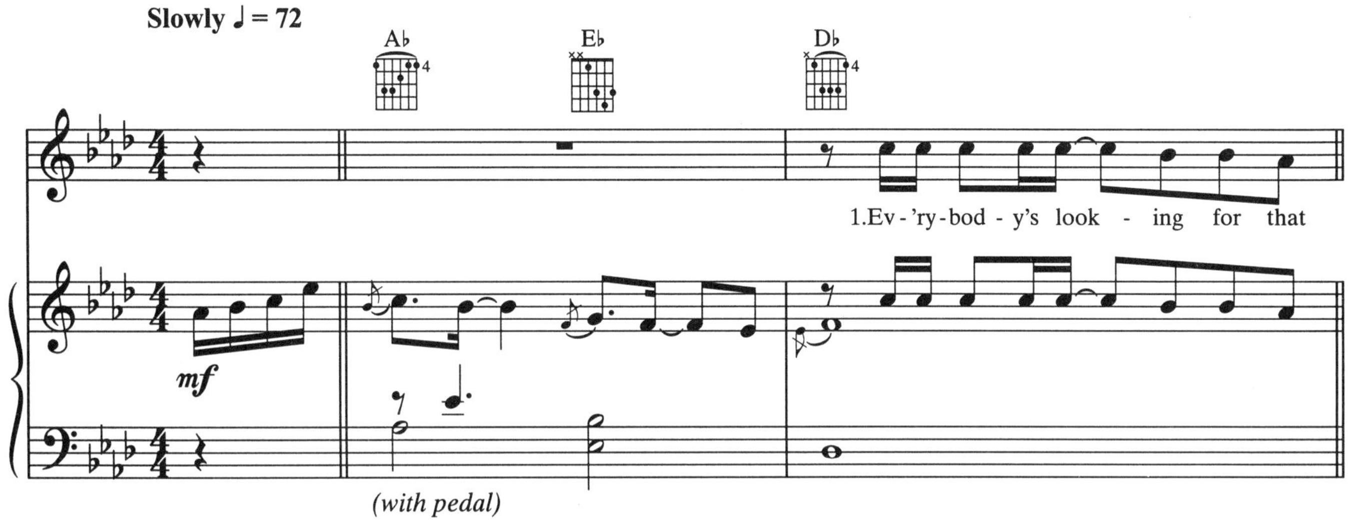

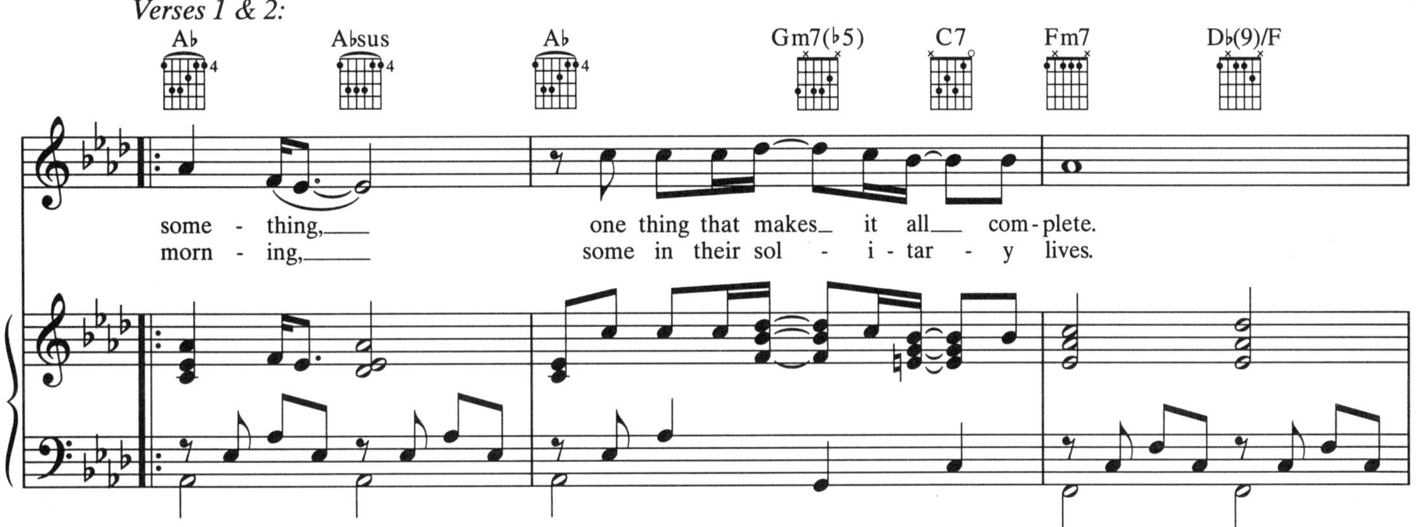

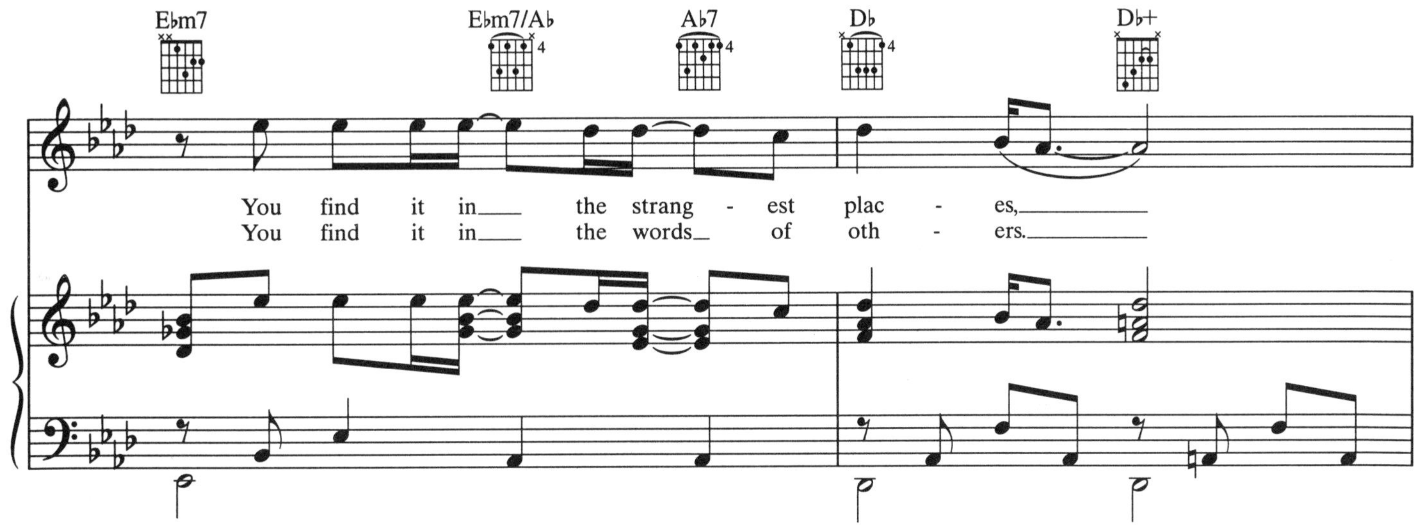

Cm7
Fm7
B♭m7
plac - es you knew__ it nev. - er could be.
A sim-ple line could make__ you laugh__ or__ cry.
B♭m7/E♭
E♭/G
A♭
A♭sus
Some find it in__ the fac - es of their chil - dren,
You find it in__ the deep - est friend - ships,
A♭
Gm7(♭5)
C7
Fm7
D♭(9)/F
Fm7
E♭
some find it in__ their lov - er's__ eyes.
the kind you cher - ish all__ your__ life.
Who can de - ny__ the joy__ it
And when you know__ how much__ that
D♭
B♭m7/E♭
brings? When you find that spe - cial thing, you're fly - ing with - out
means, you've found that spe - cial thing. You're fly - ing with - out

1.
2.
A♭ A♭sus A♭ N.C. A♭ B♭m7 A♭/C
wings. 2. Some find it shar - ing ev - 'ry So im - pos - si -
wings.
Bridge:
D♭maj7 D♭+ D♭6 B♭/D E♭ C7/E Fm7 E♭/G
ble as they may seem, you've got to fight for ev - 'ry
A♭ E♭/A♭ Fm/A♭ D♭maj7 D♭m6 B♭♭9/D
dream. 'Cause who's to know which one you let go would have
B♭m7/E♭
made you com - plete. 3. But for me, it's wak - ing up be - side

Verse 3:
Ab
Absus
Ab
Gm7(b5)
C7
Fm7
Db(9)/F
you
to watch the sun - rise on your face,
Ebm7
Ebm7/Ab
Ab7
Db
Db+
to know that I can say I love you
Cm7
Fm7
Bbm7
Bbm7/Eb
at an - y giv - en time or place.
It's the lit - tle things that on -
Ab
Absus
Ab
Gm7(b5)
C7
Fm7
Db(9)/F
ly I know,
those are the things that make you mine.

Fm7
E♭
D♭
B♭m7/E♭
And it's like fly - ing with-out wings, 'cause you're my spe-cial thing. I'm fly-ing with-out
A♭
A♭sus
A♭
D♭
B♭7/D
wings.
You're the place my life be-gins and you'll be where it
B♭m7/E♭
D♭
B♭7/D
B♭m7/E♭
ends. I'm fly-ing with-out wings and that's the joy it brings. I'm fly-ing with-out
rit.
N.C.
A♭
A♭7/C
D♭m6
A♭
wings.

From the Twentieth Century Fox Motion Picture "ONE FINE DAY"

FOR THE FIRST TIME

Words and Music by
JAMES NEWTON HOWARD,
ALLAN RICH and JUD FRIEDMAN

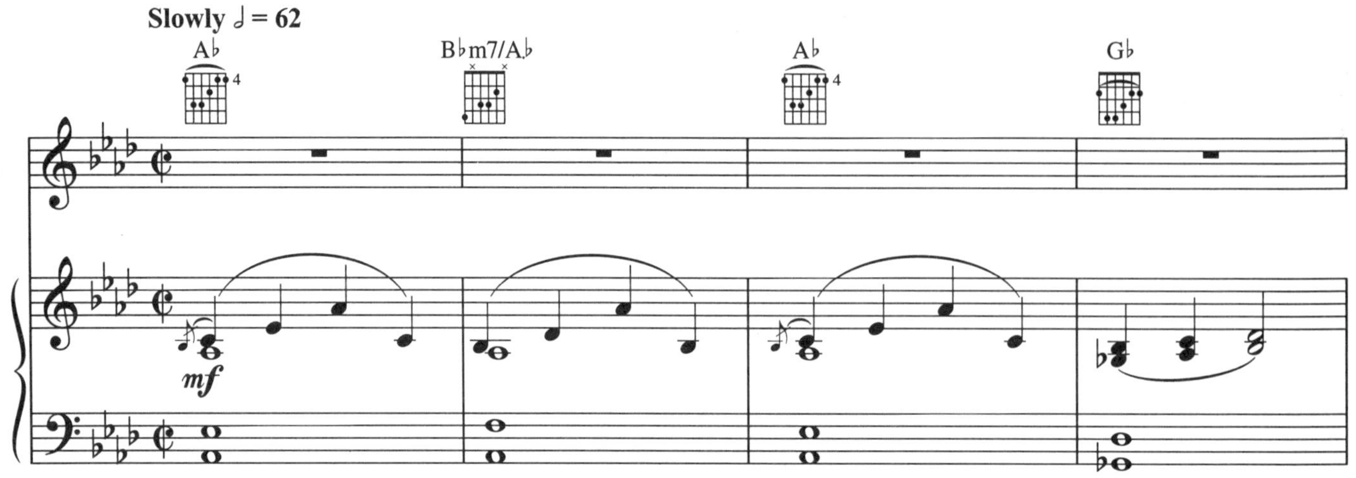

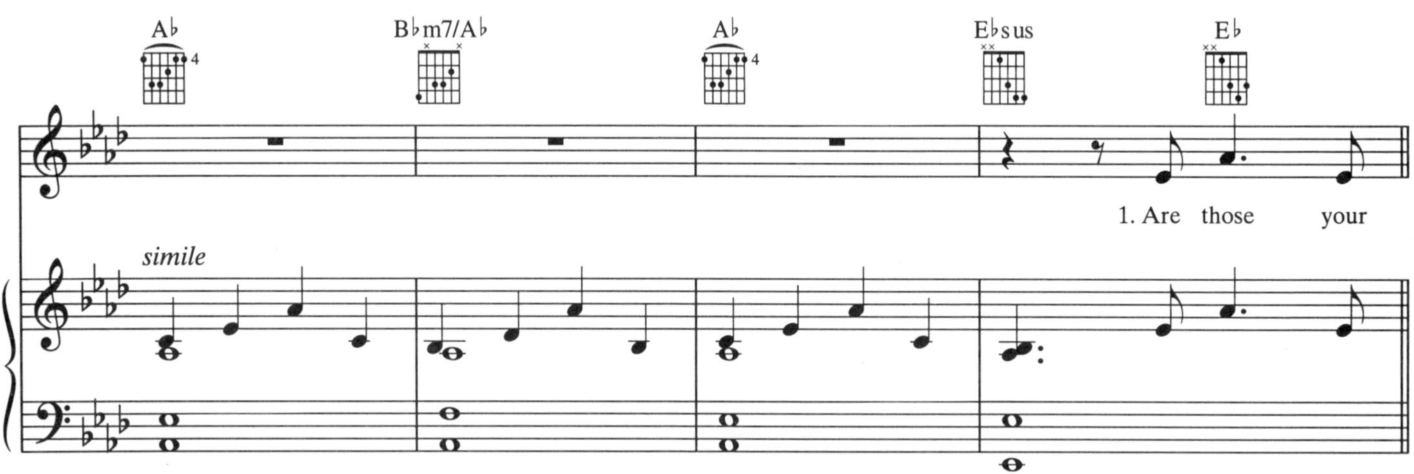

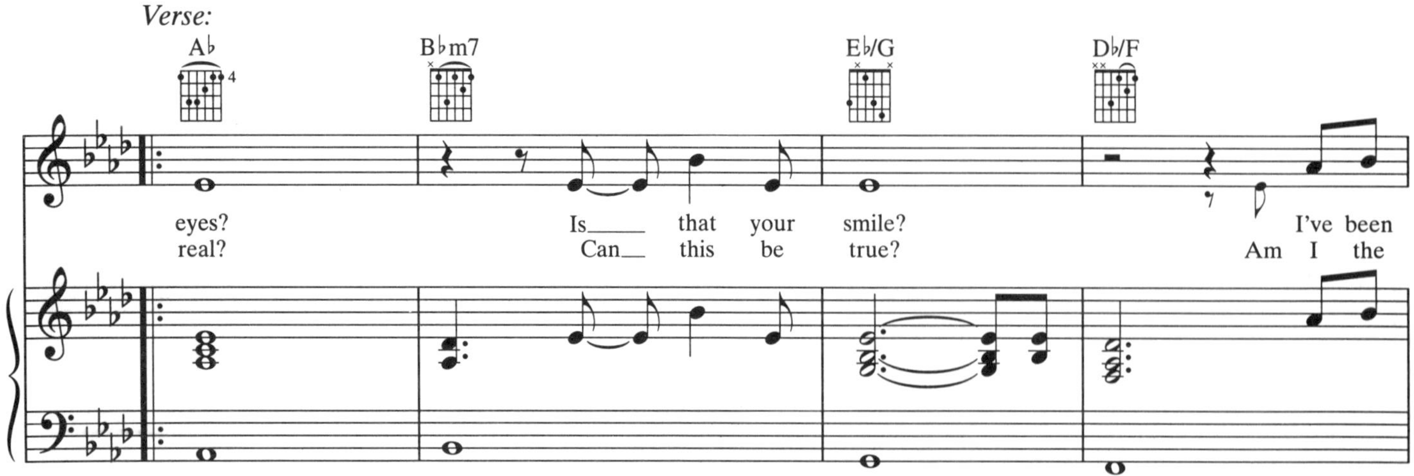

Ab Fm7 Bbm7 Ebsus Eb

look-ing at you for-ev-er, yet I nev-er saw you be-fore. Are these your
per-son I was this morn-ing, and are you the same you? It's all so

Ab Db/F Ab/C Db

hands hold-ing mine? Now I
strange. How can it be? All a-

Fm Db Ebsus Eb

won-der how I could-'ve been so blind. } And for the
long, this love was right in front of me. }

Chorus:

Ab Dbmaj9 Fm7 Eb/G

first time, I am look-ing in your eyes. For the

A♭ D♭ E♭sus E♭
first time, I'm see - ing who you are. I can't be - lieve
D♭/F D♭m/F♭ A♭/E♭ D♭ D♭m6
how much I see when you're look - ing back at me. Now I
A♭/E♭ Fm7 B♭m7 E♭sus E♭
un - der - stand what love is, love is for the
1.
A♭ Fm7 D♭maj9 E♭sus E♭
first time. 2. Can this be

2.

Bridge:

Ebsus
Eb
Bbm7
Fm7
Bbm7
Such a long time ago, I had given up on
Ebsus
Eb
Ab
Eb/G
Fm7
finding this emotion ever again.
Eb/G
Ab
Dm7(b5)
G7(#5 b9)
But you're here with me now, yes, I found you somehow,
G7(#5)
Cm7
Fsus
and I've never been so sure.

F
B♭
Cm7/B♭
B♭
a tempo
Chorus:
A♭
B♭
E♭maj9
Gm7
And for the first time, I am look - ing in your eyes.
F/A
B♭
E♭
Fsus
For the first time, I'm see - ing who you are.
F
E♭/G
E♭m/G♭
B♭/F
I can't be - lieve how much I see when you're look - ing back at me.

E♭
E♭m6
B♭/F
Gm7
Now I un - der - stand what love is,

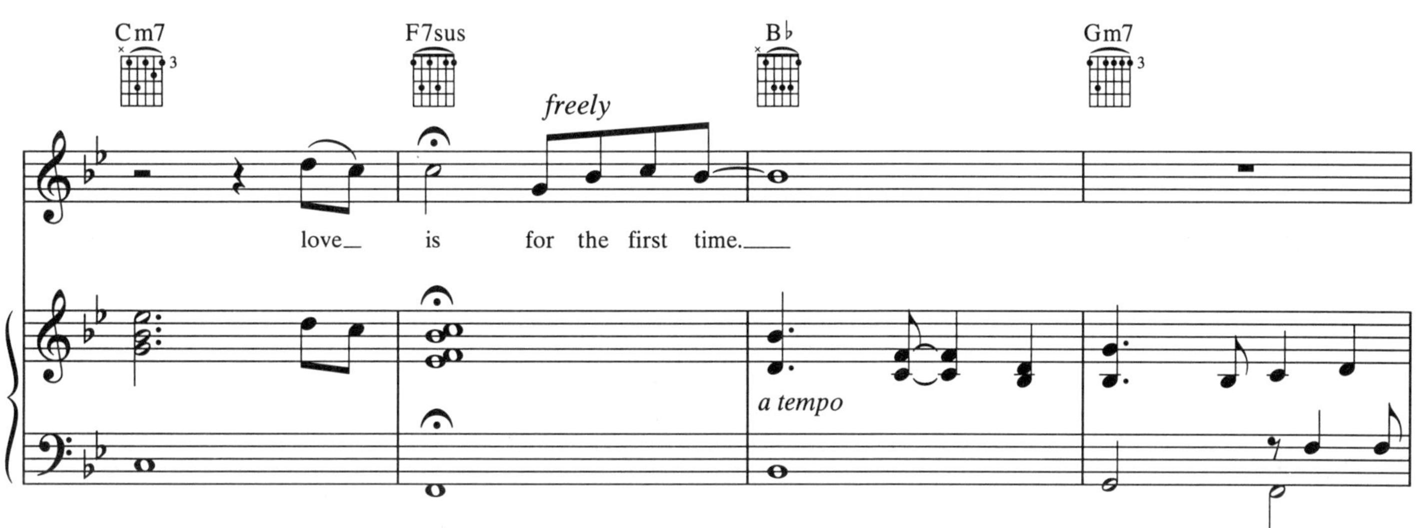
Cm7
F7sus
B♭
Gm7
freely
love is for the first time.
a tempo

E♭maj9
F7sus
B♭
rit.

FOREVER AND FOR ALWAYS

Words and Music by
SHANIA TWAIN and R.J. LANGE

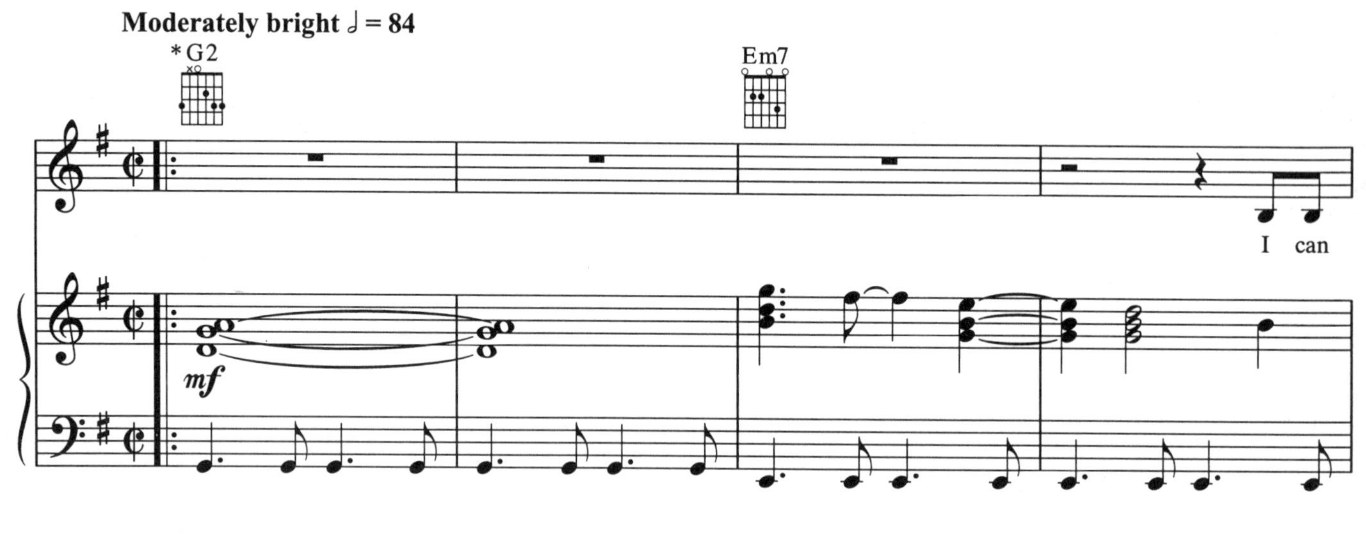

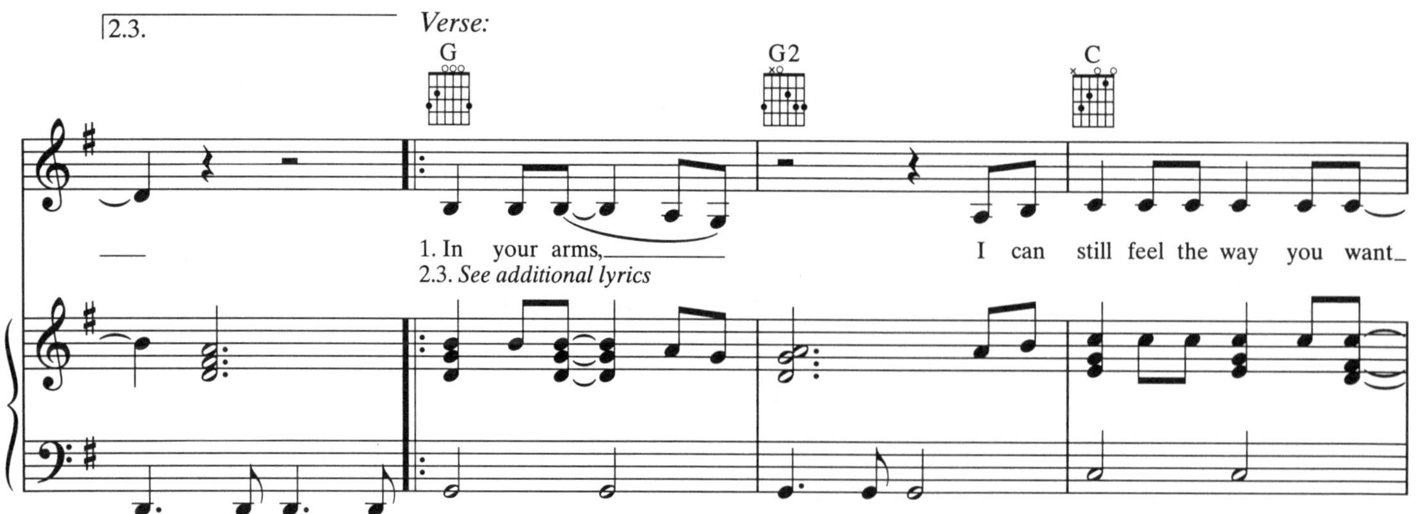

* Original recording down a 1/2 step in F♯.

D
G
A7sus
C
me when you hold me.
I can still hear the words you whis-
pered when you told me
I can stay right here for - ev -
er in your arms.
And there ain't no way
I'm let - tin' you go now.
And there ain't no way

A7sus
C
D
Em7
and there ain't no how, I'll nev - er see that day.
G(9)/B
Am
D
Chorus:
G
'Cause I'm keep - ing you for - ev -
C
G
er and for al - ways.
We will be to - geth -
C
D
er all of our days.
Wan - na wake up ev - 'ry morn -

Am
C
To Coda
G
ing to your sweet face, al - ways.
G(9)/B
Em7
1.
2.
D.C. al Coda
C
D
Coda
G
I'm keep - ing you for - ev - er and for

C
G
al - ways.
We will be to - geth - er all of
C
D
Am
our days.
Wan-na wake up ev - 'ry morn - ing to your
C
D
Am
sweet face.
I'm keep - ing you for - ev - er and for
G
G(9)/B
al - ways.

Verse 2:
In your heart,
I can still hear a beat for everytime you kiss me.
And when we're apart,
I know how much you miss me,
I can feel your love for me in your heart.

And there ain't no way
I'm lettin' you go now.
And there ain't no way
And there ain't no how,
I'll never see that day.
(To Chorus:)

Verse 3:
In your eyes,
I can still see the look of the one who really loves me.
The one who wouldn't put anything else
In the world above me.
I can still see the love for me in your eyes.

And there ain't no way
I'm lettin' you go now.
And there ain't no way
And there ain't no how,
I'll never see that day.
(To Chorus:)

FOREVER I DO
(The Wedding Song)

Words and Music by
CYNTHIA BIGGS and DEXTER WANSEL

D
Bm9
F♯m7
G
stand here in the eyes of the be - hold - ers,
Em7
D
G/A
D
to - geth - er.
Do I
Do I
F♯m7
Gmaj7
Asus
D
take you this mo - ment,
prom - ise to love you?
and _ for my
And _ for my
C/D
D/F♯
G(add9)
E/G♯
F♯7
whole life through?
whole life through,
Do I prom - ise to
do I take you from this

Bm7
2fr
D7/A
G
3
love you?
mo - ment?
For - ev - er I do,
G/A
D
A/C♯
for - ev - er I do.
For -
F♯m7
Bm7
2fr
F/G
ev - er I do; I'll al - ways love
Em7/A
F♯m7
Bm7
2fr
you. For - ev - er I do; I

F/G
Em7/A
F♯m7
Bm7
promise to be true. For - ev - er I do; I'll
F/G
F♯7sus
F♯7/A♯
Bm7
E7/G♯
al - ways be by your side. For - ev - er I
G(add9)
G/A
D
G/B
A/C♯
do, for - ev - er I do.
freely
a tempo
D
D/F♯
G(add9)
D/F♯
G(add9)
G/A
G(add9)
G/A
D
This band of
rit.
rit.

FROM THIS MOMENT ON

Words and Music by
SHANIA TWAIN and R.J. LANGE

D/F♯
D/G
G
for better, for worse, I will love you with ev - 'ry beat of my heart.
C
D
G/C
1. From this
Slowly ♩ = 72
Verse 1:
G5
C (9)
mo - ment life has be - gun. From this mo - ment
D5
C (9)
G5
you are the one. Right be - side you is where I be - long,

Am
D
G5
Verse 2:
from this mo - ment on.
2. From this mo - ment I have been blessed.
C (9)
D5
I live on - ly for your hap - pi - ness. And for your
C (9)
G5
Am
D
love I'd give my last breath, from this mo - ment on.
Chorus:
C (9)
G
C (9)
I give my hand to you with all my heart. Can't

D G

wait to live__ my life__ with you,_ can't wait to start._ You and I___ will nev - er be__ a -

C (9) Em7 C (9)

part.________ My dreams__ came true________________ be - cause_

G G/D D N.C. *Verse 3:* A (9) E

__ of you.______________ 3. From this mo - ment, as long as I live,_

D E

___ I will love you,____________ I prom - ise you this.________ There is noth-

D
A
Bm
E
ing I would - n't give, from this mo - ment on.
D(9)
A
F♯m7
D(9)
E
Chorus:
A
You're the rea - son I be - lieve in
D
E
love. And you're the an - swer to my prayers from

A
up a - bove.
All we need is just the two of
D
F♯m7
D(9)
us.
My dreams came true be - cause
A
A/E
E
N.C.
of you.
4. From this
Verse 4:
B
mo - ment, as long as I live, I will

E
F♯
E
love you, I prom-ise you this. There is noth-ing I would-n't give,
B
C♯m
F♯
E(9)
from this mo-ment. I will love you, I will love you as
B
C♯m
E
long as I live, from this mo - ment
E(9)
B/D♯
F♯7
B
on.
on.
Mm, mm.
rit.

THE HAWAIIAN WEDDING SONG

KE KALI NEI AU

English Words by
AL HOFFMAN and DICK MANNING
Hawaiian Words and Music
by CHARLES E. KING

*Symbols for Guitar, Diagrams for Ukulele.

*Small notes for duet version with girl.

C
Ah
Ah
Ah
I will love you long - er than for - ev - er.
Ka - 'u ia e le - i a - e ne - i la
Me ke a - la pu - a pi - ka - ke
F
D7
G7
My dar - ling, My love.
No' ka i - ini Wale no
O oe kuu pua le hua
Now that we are one, Clouds won't hide the sun. Blue
Nou no ka i - ini A nou wa - le no A
A o oe kuu pua kuu pua lei le - hua A'u
C
A7
D7
G7
C
skies of Ha - wai - i smile on this, our wed - ding day. I
o ko a - lo - ha ka'u e hi - i - po - i mau Na'u
e li - 'a ma - u nei hoo - paa ia iho kea - loha. He
A7
D7
G7
1. C
G7
2. C
I do love you
(opt.)
do love you with all my heart. heart.
oe na'u oe, e lei e lei, na'u oe e lei. lei.
lei, he lei, oe na'u, oe na'u, he lei oe na'u. na'u.
mf

HERE AND NOW

Words and Music by
TERRY STEELE and DAVID ELLIOT

1.
C
G2/B
D♯dim7
Em
G2/B
C(2)
C/D
Hold-ing you close through the night,
I need you.

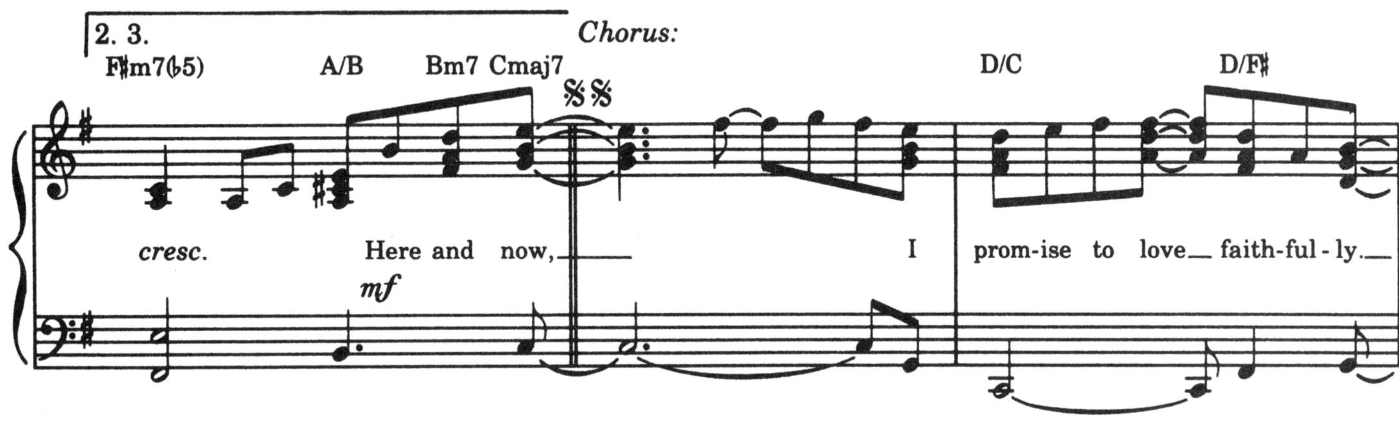
2. 3.
Chorus:
F♯m7(♭5)
A/B
Bm7
Cmaj7
D/C
D/F♯
cresc.
Here and now,
I
prom-ise to love faith-ful-ly.
mf

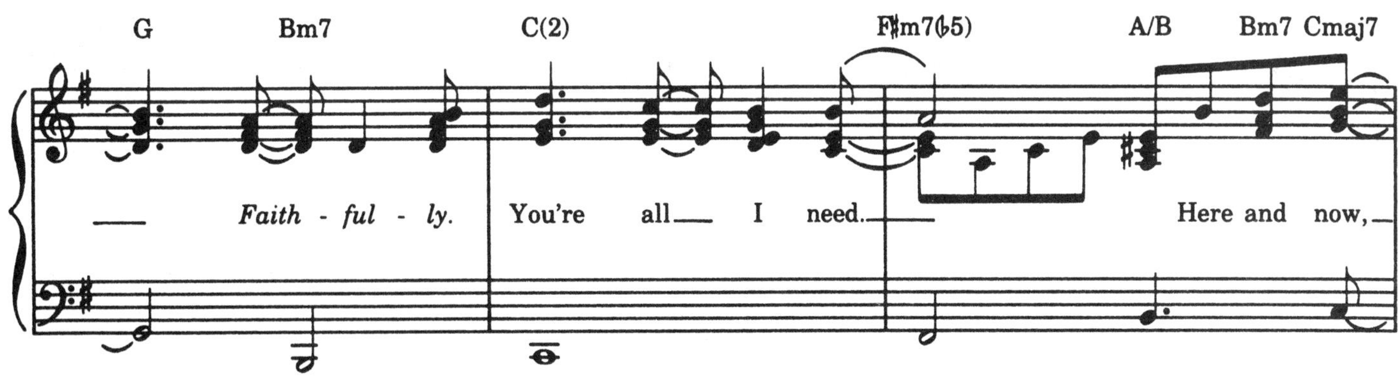
G
Bm7
C(2)
F♯m7(♭5)
A/B
Bm7
Cmaj7
Faith - ful - ly.
You're all I need.
Here and now,

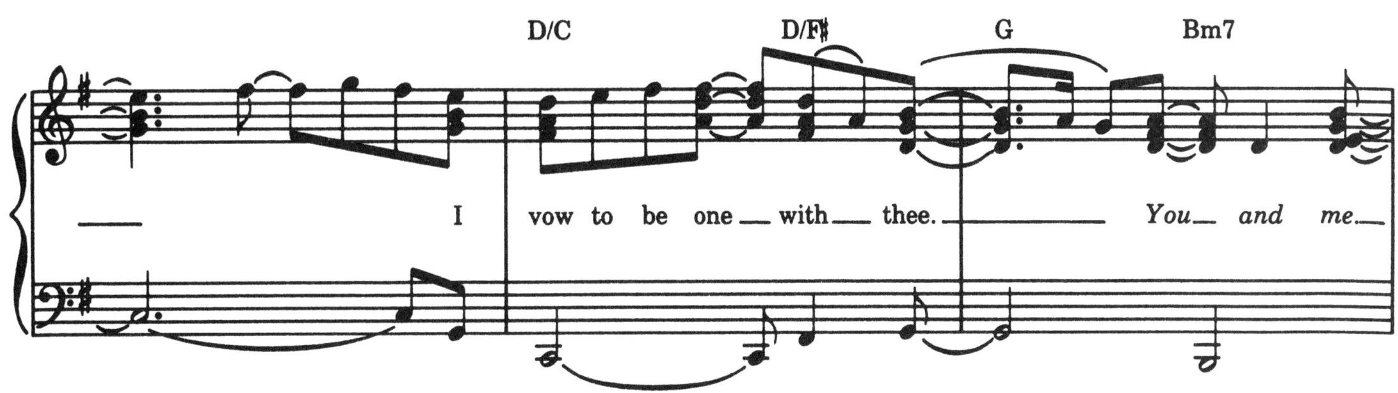
D/C
D/F♯
G
Bm7
I
vow to be one with thee.
You and me

Cmaj9
To Coda
1.
C(2)
C/D
G
G(2)/B
Your love is all I need.

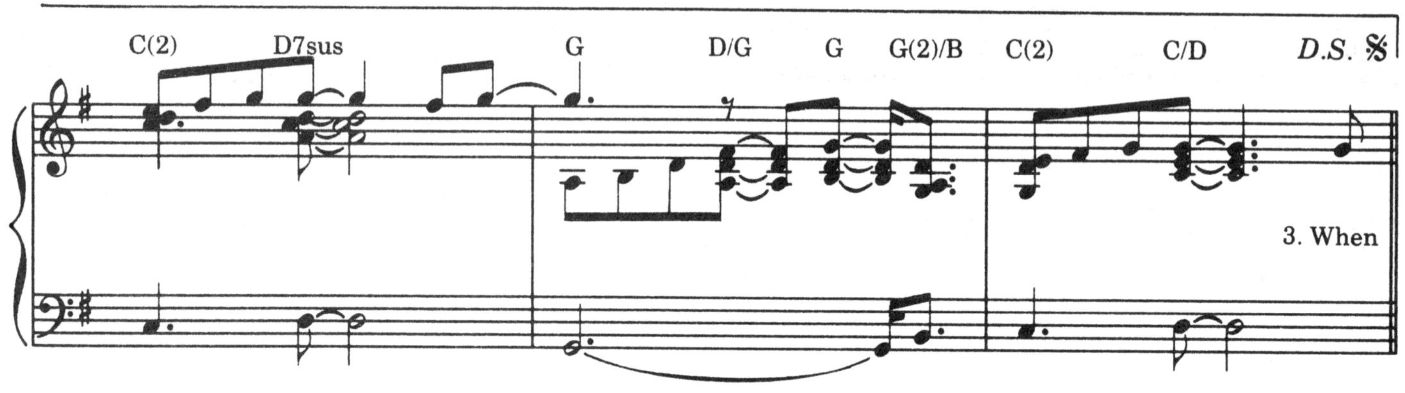
C(2)
D7sus
G
D/G
G
G(2)/B
C(2)
C/D
D.S.
3. When

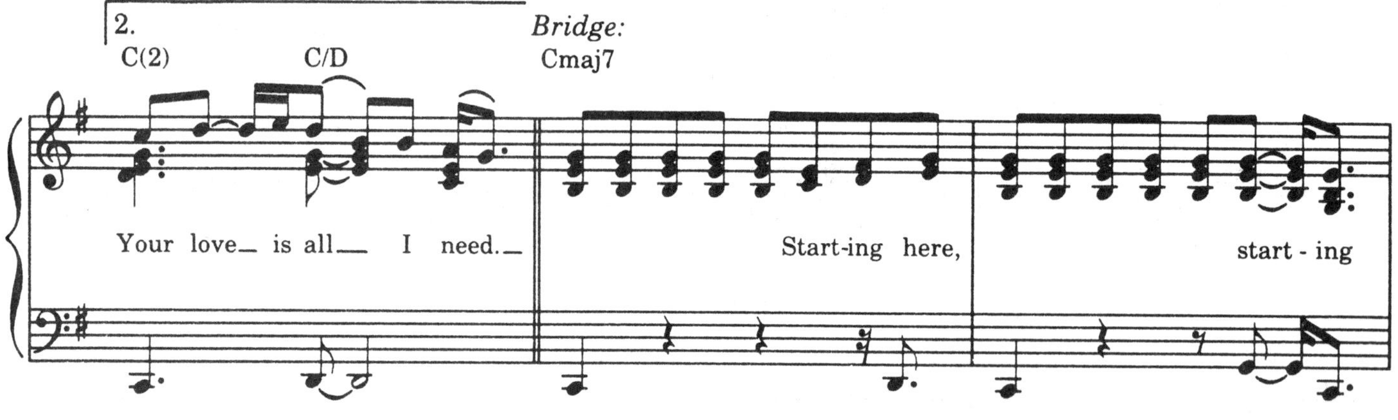
2.
C(2)
C/D
Bridge:
Cmaj7
Your love is all I need.
Start-ing here,
start - ing

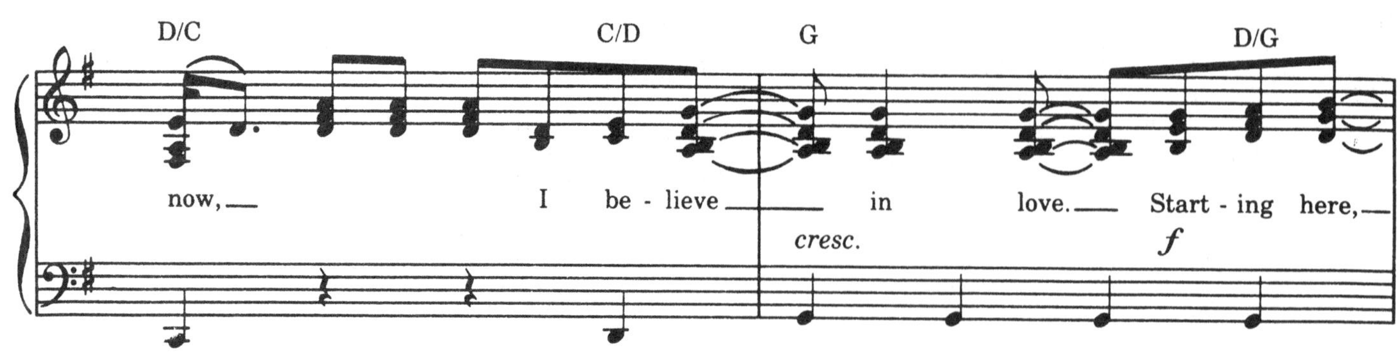
D/C
C/D
G
D/G
now,
I be - lieve
in
love.
Start - ing here,
cresc.
f

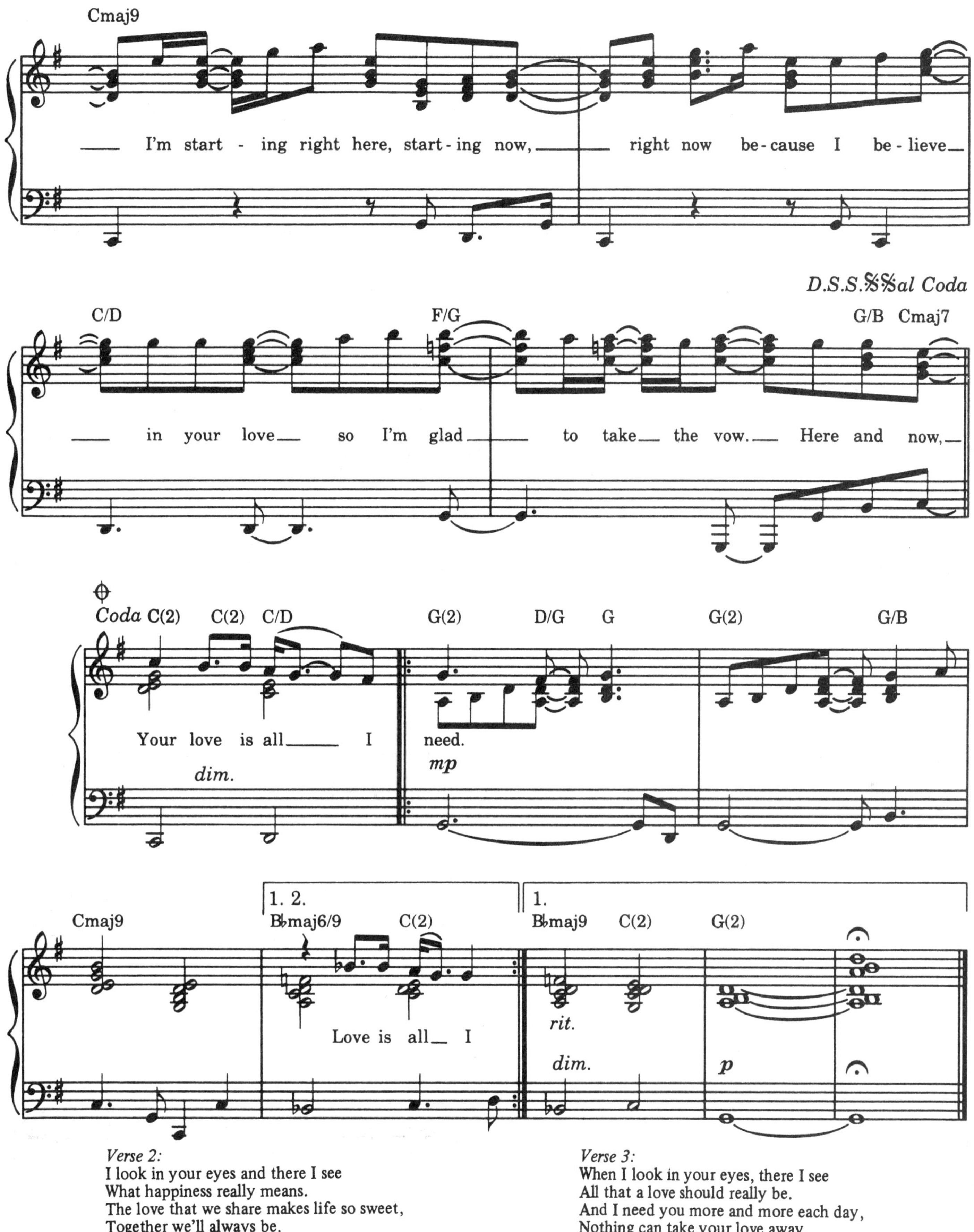

Verse 2:
I look in your eyes and there I see
What happiness really means.
The love that we share makes life so sweet,
Together we'll always be.
This pledge of love feels so right,
And ooh, I need you.
To Chorus:

Verse 3:
When I look in your eyes, there I see
All that a love should really be.
And I need you more and more each day,
Nothing can take your love away.
More than I dare to dream,
I need you.
To Chorus:

I BELIEVE IN YOU AND ME

Words and Music by
SANDY LINZER and DAVID WOLFERT

B
Bmaj7
D♯m7/G♯
G♯m7
D♯m7
you will al - ways be the one for me. Oh, yes, you will.
C♯m7
C♯m7/F♯
B
B/A
And I be-lieve in dreams a - gain. I be-lieve that love will nev-er end. And
E(9)/G♯
Em7
A9
B/F♯
like the riv - er finds the sea, I was lost, now I'm
D♯m7
G♯m7
C♯m7
C♯m7/F♯
1.
B
C♯m7/F♯
N.C.
free, 'cause I be - lieve in you and me. 2. I will nev - er leave

2.
Bridge:
B
D♯m7
G♯m7
D♯m7
G♯m7
me.
May-be I'm a fool to feel the way I do.
mf
C♯m7
C♯m(maj7)
C♯m7
C♯m7/F♯
N.C.
Dm7/G
I would play the fool for-ev-er just to be with you for-ev-er.
3. I be-lieve in
Verse 3:
C
C/B♭
Fmaj9
mir-a-cles, and love's a mir-a-cle.
And yes, ba-by, you're my dream come true.
Fm7/B♭
A♭/B♭
B♭/A♭
Fmaj7
C/G
Em7
Am7
I was lost, now I'm free,
oh ba-by, 'cause

Dm7 C/E Dm7/G N.C. B♭maj7/C *freely* C Fmaj9

I believe, I do believe in you and me. See I'm lost, now I'm

Em7 Am7 Dm7 Dm7/G N.C.

free, 'cause I be-lieve in you and me,

a tempo

C C/B♭ Fmaj9 Dm7 Dm7/G C

be-lieve in you and me.

rit.

Verse 2:
I will never leave your side,
I will never hurt your pride.
When all the chips are down,
I will always be around,
Just to be right where you are, my love.
Oh, I love you, boy.
I will never leave you out,
I will always let you in
To places no one has ever been.
Deep inside, can't you see?
I believe in you and me.
(To Bridge:)

From the Motion Picture "THE MIRROR HAS TWO FACES"

I FINALLY FOUND SOMEONE

Words and Music by
BARBRA STREISAND, MARVIN HAMLISCH,
R.J. LANGE and BRYAN ADAMS

Emaj9
Em6
I fi - n'lly found the one___ that makes me feel com - plete.
B (9)
G♯m7
It start - ed o - ver cof - fee, we start - ed out as friends.
C♯m7/F♯
It's fun - ny how, from sim - ple things,_ the best things be - gin.
A♭(9)
Fm7
This time, it's dif - f'rent, it's all be - cause of you._

D♭maj9 D♭m6

It's bet-ter than it's ev - er been 'cause we can talk it {through. / through, yeah.}

A♭(9) Fm7

My fa-v'rite line was, "Can I call you some - time?"

D♭maj9 D♭m6

It's all you had to say to take my breath a - way.

Chorus:

F(9)

This is it! Oh, I fi - n'lly

mf

B♭maj9
B♭m6
F(9)
found some - one, some - one to share my life. I fi - n'lly
B♭maj9
B♭m6
F(9)
found the one to be with ev - 'ry night. 'Cause what -
A7sus
A7
Dm
D♭
ev - er I do, it's just got to be you. My
F/C
B♭/C
life has just be - gun, I fi - n'lly found some - one.

F(9)
Dm7
Ooh, some - one,
I fi - n'lly found some - one.
B♭maj9
F/G
Ooh,
Verse 2:
C(9)
Am7
I did - n't mind.
Ba - by, that's fine,
2. Did I keep you wait - ing?
I a - pol - o - gize.
Fmaj9
Fm6
just to know you were mine.
I will wait for - ev - er just to know you were mine.
You know,

C (9)
Am7
Are you sure it looks right?
Is - n't it too tight?
I love your hair,
I love what you wear.
Fmaj9
Fm6
I can't wait for the rest of my life!
Well, you're ex - cep - tion - al!
Chorus:
G♭(9)
This is it! Oh, I fi - n'lly
C♭maj9
C♭m6
G♭(9)
found some - one, some - one to share my life. I fi - n'lly

C♭maj9
C♭m6
G♭(9)
found the one to be with ev - 'ry night. 'Cause what -
B♭7sus
B♭7
E♭m
ev - er I do, it's just got to be you.
D
G♭/D♭
Oh yeah, my life has just be - gun, I fi - n'lly
A♭m7/D♭
E♭7sus
E♭7
found some - one. And what -

A♭m7
G♭/B♭
ev - er I do, it's just got to be you. Ooh, my
A♭m7/D♭
life has just be - gun, I fi - n'lly
G♭(9)
C♭maj9
found some - one.
G♭(9)

I CROSS MY HEART

Words and Music by
STEVE DORFF and ERIC KAZ

Fm7
E♭/G
A♭
4fr.
From here on af - ter let's stay the way we are right now.
B♭
Fm7
E♭/G
And share all the love and laugh - ter that a
D♭
4fr.
B♭7sus4
B♭7
3
life - time will al - low.
E♭
E♭/G
A♭
4fr.
B♭
f
I cross my heart and prom - ise to

E♭
E♭/G
A♭
4fr.
give all I've got to give to make all
A♭/B♭
B♭7
E♭
E♭/G
your dreams come true.
In all the
A♭
B♭
B♭/A♭
E♭/G
A♭
E♭/G
world
you'll nev - er find
a love as
Fm7
B♭7
To Coda
1.
E♭
true as mine.
mp

A♭
E♭/G
Fm7
B♭7
E♭
4fr.
You will
2.
E♭
A♭
E♭/G
mine.
And if a - long the way we find a day
Fm7
B♭7
E♭
G♭
it starts to storm. You've got the prom - ise of my love
D♭/F
E♭m7
6fr.
G♭/A♭
A♭/B♭
D.S. al Coda
to keep you warm.

Additional Lyrics

2. You will always be the miracle
   That makes my life complete.
   And as long as there's a breath in me
   I'll make yours just as sweet.
   As we look into the future,
   It's as far as we can see.
   So let's make each tomorrow
   Be the best that it can be.
   (To Chorus)

I ONLY WANT TO BE WITH YOU

Words and Music by
MIKE HAWKER and IVOR RAYMONDE

1.
2.
I only-ly want to be with you. It
I on-ly want to be with you.
D7 D C D Am7 D7 G C D G C G
You stopped and smiled at me, Asked if I'd care to dance.
Eb G C G
I fell in-to your op-en arms and I did-n't stand a chance.
D Bm7 Em7 A7
Now listen honey, I just wanna be beside you ev-ry-where. As long as were to-gether honey
D7 G Em G

I don't care 'Cos you start-ed somethin' Oh can't you see that
Em C D Am7 D7
ev-er since we met you've had a hold on me. No mat-ter what you do,
G Em Am Bm Am C♯dim.
To Coda
D 𝄋 al
I on-ly want to be with you.
D7 D C D Am7 D7 G C G
Coda.
I said I on-ly want to be with you.
rall.
G C G Am7 D7 G C G

I SWEAR

Words and Music by
GARY BAKER and FRANK MYERS

G♭
E♭m7/A♭
4fr.
A♭
4fr.
D♭
4fr.
I know my part.
I'll stand
be - side
G♭/B♭
A♭/C
D♭
4fr.
G♭
A♭
4fr.
you through the years,
you'll on - ly cry
those hap - py tears.
B♭m
D♭/A♭
4fr.
E♭/G
And though I'll make
mis - takes,
I'll nev - er break
your heart.
E♭m7/A♭
4fr.
A♭
4fr.
D♭
4fr.
B♭m7
I swear,
by the moon
and the stars
in the sky,

Fm7
Gb
Ab
4fr.
Db
4fr.
I'll be there.
I swear,
like a sha-
Bbm7
Fm7
Gb
Ab
4fr.
dow that's by your side,
I'll be there.
For
Ebm7
6fr.
Ebm7/Ab
4fr.
Ab
4fr.
Ebm7
6fr.
To Coda
bet-ter or worse, till
death do us part, I'll
love you with ev - er - y beat
1.
Ebm7/Ab
4fr.
Ab
4fr.
Db
4fr.
Bbm7
of my heart, I swear.

Additional lyrics

2. I'll give you everything I can,
I'll build your dreams with these two hands,
And we'll hang some memories on the wall.
And when there's silver in your hair,
You won't have to ask if I still care,
'Cause as time turns the page my love won't age at all.
(To Chorus)

I WILL FOLLOW HIM
(I Will Follow You)

English Words by
NORMAN GIMBEL and ARTHUR ALTMAN
Original Lyric by JACQUES PLANTE
Music by J.W. STOLE and DEL ROMA

Moderately, with a beat

no chord
Eb
Fm7
mf

Bb7
no chord
Eb

I will fol - low him, ___ fol - low him wher - ev - er

Gm
Cm

he may go. ___ There is - n't an o - cean too

Gm
Ab
Bb7

deep, a moun - tain so high it can keep me a -

Eb
Cm
Eb
way.
I must fol - low him.
Gm
Ev - er since he touched my hand
I knew
that
Cm
Gm
Ab
near him I al - ways must
be,
and noth - ing can keep him from
Bb7
Eb
Bb7
me,
he is my des - tin - y.
I

Eb
Cm
love him, I love him, I love him and where he goes I'll fol-ow,
I'll fol-low, I'll
for - ev - er and
Cm
Fm7
Bb7
Eb
fol-low he'll al-ways be my true love, my true love, my true love, from now un - til for -
ev - er and side by side to - geth - er I'll be with my true love, and share a thou-sand
Cm
no chord
Eb
ev - er, for - ev - er, for - ev - er.
sun-sets to - geth - er be - side him.
I will fol - low him,
Gm
fol - low him wher - ev - er he may go. There

Cm
Gm
A♭
is - n't an o - cean too deep,
a moun - tain so high it can
Fm7
B♭7
E♭
E♭/B♭
keep, keep me a - way,
a - way from my love.
I a - way from my love.
Ah
Fm7
Cm
E♭

IF YOU LOVE ME, REALLY LOVE ME

English Words by GEOFFREY PARSONS
French Words by EDITH PIAF
Music by MARGUERITE MONNOT

If You Love Me, Really Love Me - 2 - 1

G C6 D7♭9 G Em B7 Em B7 Em
hap-pen, darl-ing, I won't care. Shall I catch a shoot-ing star? Shall I bring it where you are? If you
mour puis-que tu m'ai - mes. J'i-rais jus qu'au bout du monde, Je me fe-rais tein-dre blonde, Si tu
Rubato a bit faster
C♯dim C7 B7 C♯dim C7 B7 Am7 D7 Gmaj.7 Cmaj.7 Am6 B7 Em Em7
want me to, I will. You can set me an-y task. I'll do an-y-thing you ask, if you'll
me le de-mand-ais. On peut bien ri-re de moi, Je fe-rais n'im por-te quoi, Si tu
Am Am7 D7 G B7 Em Em7
on-ly love me still. When at last our life on earth is through, I will
me le de-man-dais Nous aur-ons pour nous l'é-ter-ni-té, Dans le
a tempo
Am Am7 D7 G B7 C Cm6
share e-ter-ni-ty with you. IF YOU LOVE ME, REAL-LY LOVE ME, then what-
bleu de toute l'im-men-si-té Dans le ciel plus de pro-blé-mes, Dieu ré-
G Am7 D7♭9 1. G D7 2. G Cm6 D7♭9 G6
ev-er hap-pens, I won't care. If the care.
u-nit ceux qui s'ai - ment. Le ciel ment.
rit. a tempo mf rall.
Ped. *

I'LL ALWAYS LOVE YOU

Words and Music by
JIMMY GEORGE

Cmaj9
Am7
Dm7
F/G
love you for the rest of my days.
love you for all that you are.
Instrumental
You have won my
You have made my
heart and my soul with your sweet sex-
life com-plete. You're my luck-
-y ways.
-y star.
end instrumental
B♭/C
C7
You gave me hope
You are the one
You gave my world

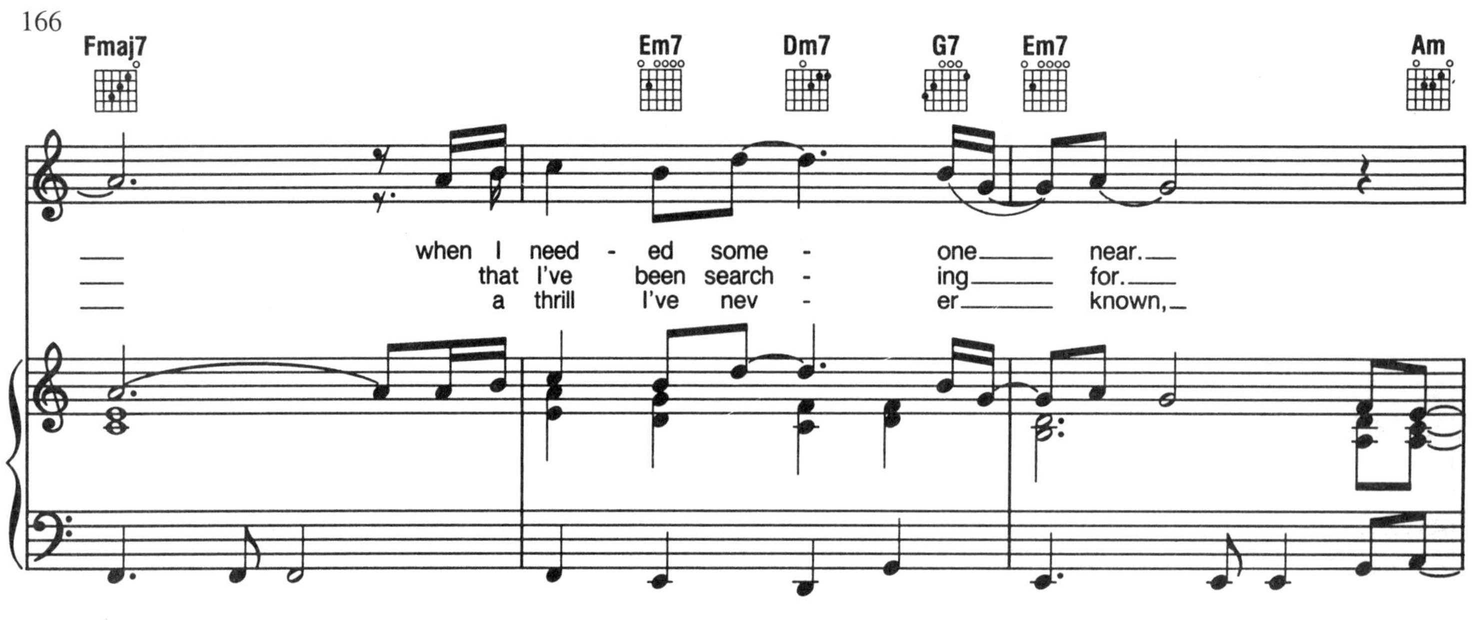
Fmaj7
Em7
Dm7
G7
Em7
Am
when I need - ed some - one near.
that I've been search - ing for.
a thrill I've nev - er known,

Dm7
You bring me hap - pi - ness ev - 'ry
You are my ev - 'ry - thing. Tell me,
and filled my ea - ger heart with a

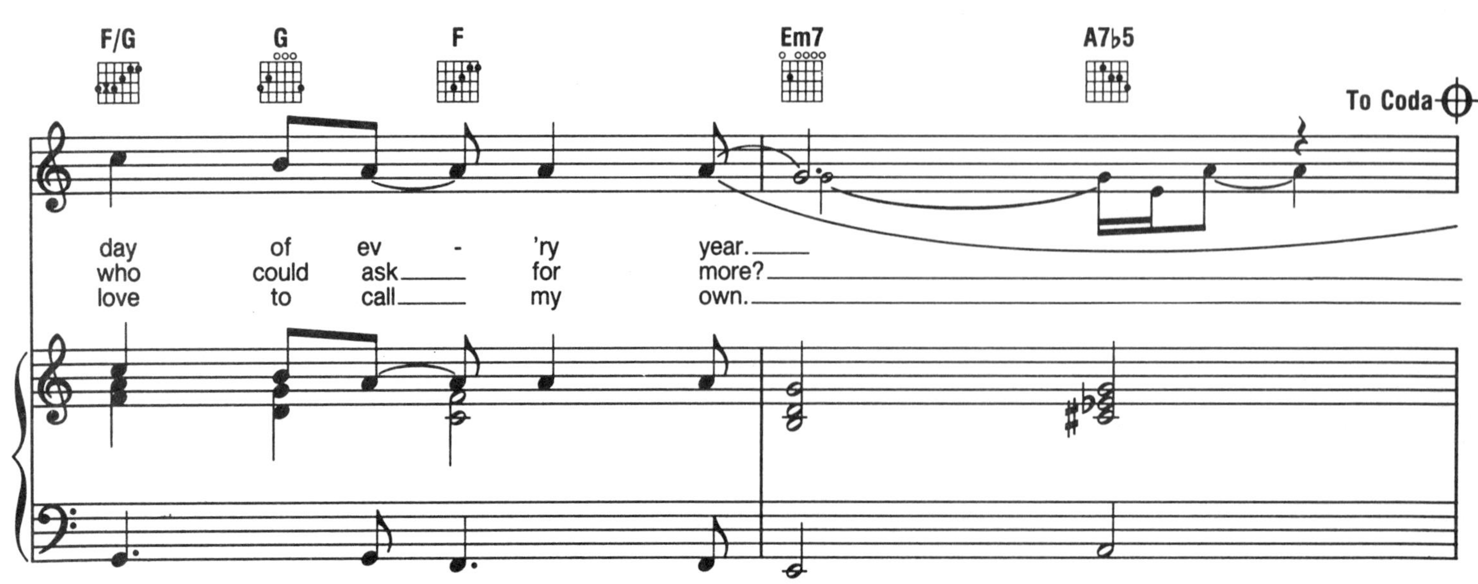
F/G
G
F
Em7
A7♭5
To Coda
day of ev - 'ry year.
who could ask for more?
love to call my own.

1
Ab maj7
F/G
And I'll al - ways
2
Fm9
Fm/Bb
And I'll al - ways love
Eb
you.
Cm7
Hon - ey, this will
Fm7
never end.
Ab/Bb
I need you by my
Eb
side, ba - by.
Cm7
You're my lov - er, my friend.

Dm7
F/G
D.S. al Coda
Oh, my friend.
CODA
Fm9
Fm/B♭
E♭
E♭/G
And I'll al - ways love you.
Cm7
Fm9
A♭/B♭
You must know how much I do.
You can
E♭
Cm7
count on me for - ev - er
and I will take good

Fm7
Ab/Bb
care of you.
I'll al - ways love
Gbmaj9
Ebm7
you.
Oh, I'm so hap - py
Abm7
Cb/Db
Gb
that you're mine.
I'll al - ways love
you
Ebm7
Abm7
Db
un - til the end of time.

Ebmaj9 Cm7/Bb Bb6

Fmaj7/G Cmaj7

Oo.

Cm7/Bb Bb

Ah.

Fmaj7/G Cmaj7

Repeat ad lib. and Fade

Oh, yeah. Oh, yeah. Oo.

I'M ALIVE

Words and Music by
KRISTIAN LUNDIN and ANDREAS CARLSSON

Moderately ♩ = 104

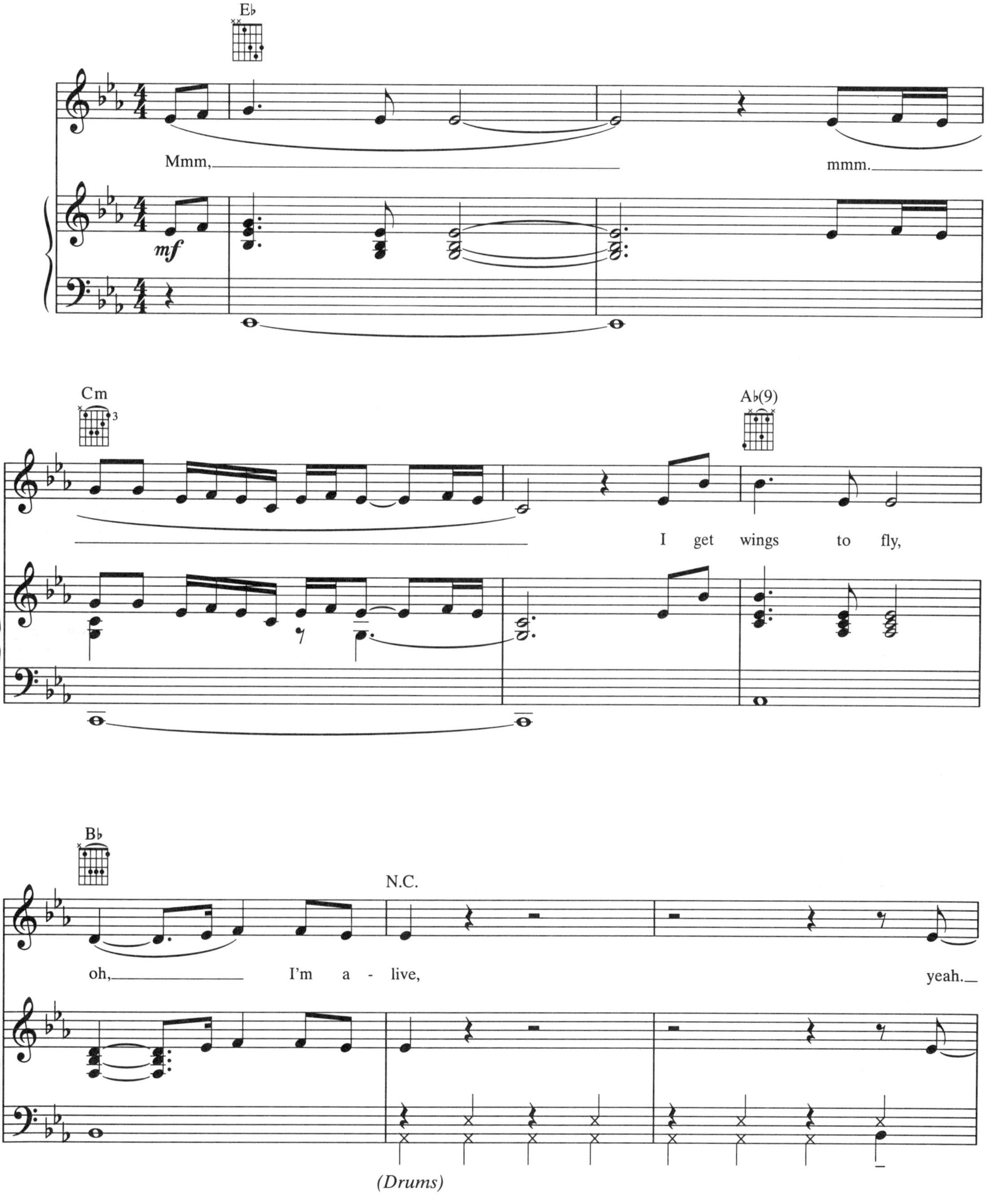

E♭

Mmm, mmm.

mf

Cm

A♭(9)

I get wings to fly,

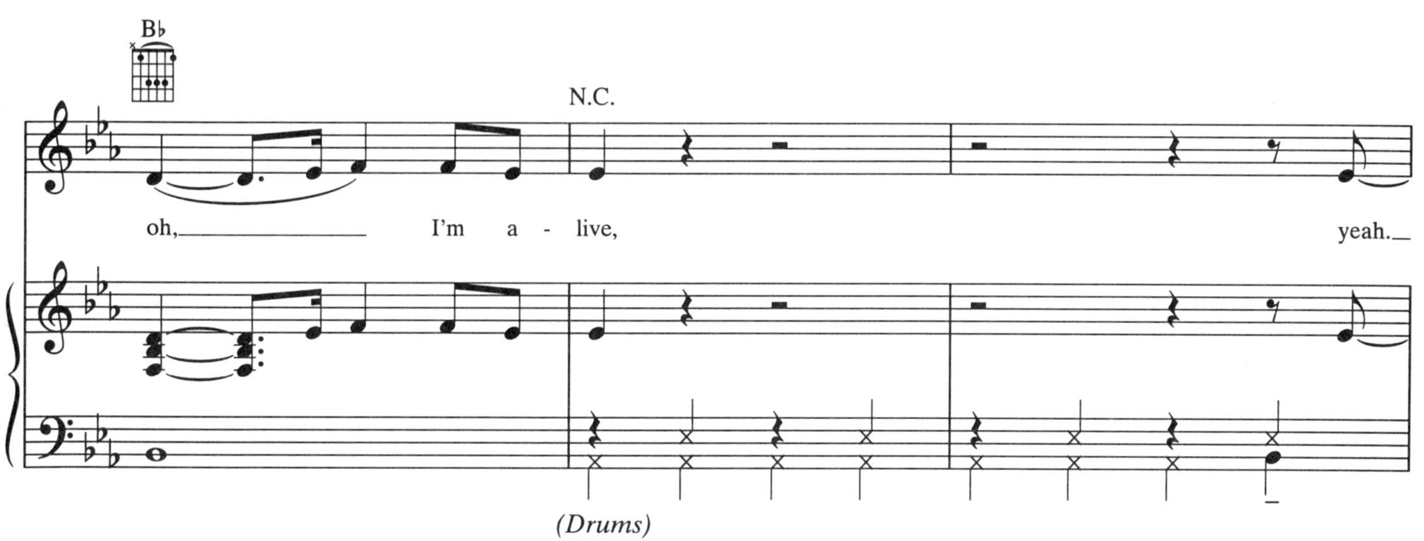

simile
Chorus:
E♭
When you call on me, when I
Cm
hear you breathe,
A♭(9)
I get wings to fly. I
B♭
feel that I'm a - live.
E♭
When you

To Coda 

Cm
A♭(9)
look at me I can touch the sky. I
reach for me raising spirits high, God
B♭
E♭
know that I'm alive. Oh,
Cm
A♭
woh, oh.
B♭
E♭
When you bless the day I just

Cm
Ab(9)
drift a - way.
All my wor - ries die, I'm
Bb
Eb
glad that I'm a - live.
You've
Verse:
Cm
Ab
set my heart on fire,
filled me with love,
made me a wom-
Bb
Eb
an on clouds a - bove,
yeah. I

Cm
could - n't get much high - er, my spir - it takes flight,
A♭
B♭
D.S.𝄋 al Coda
'cause I'm a - live, oh. When you
Coda
E♭
B♭
Bridge:
Fm
Fm7
knows that, that I'll be the one stand - ing
Cm
B♭
3
by through good and through try - ing times.

D♭
Fm
E♭
And it's on - ly__ be - gun.__ I____ can't wait for__ the rest of__ my
B♭
N.C.
Chorus:
F
life.__ (When you call on me,) When you
Dm
call on__ me,____ (when you reach for me,) when__ you reach for__ me,____ (I get
B♭(9)
C
F
wings to fly. I feel____ that...__) (When you bless the day,) When you bless,__

Dm
you bless the day, (I just drift a - way.) I just drift a - way. (All my
B♭(9)
C
Dm
wor - ries die.) I know that I'm a - live, yeah, yeah, yeah.
B♭(9)
I get wings to fly, God
C
F
knows that I'm a - live.
rit.

THE IRISH WEDDING SONG

(The Wedding Song)

Words and Music by
IAN BETTERIDGE

Moderate, gentle waltz

E♭ B♭ F7 B♭ Verse

mp

1.(T) Here they
2. May they
3. As they

B♭ E♭ B♭

stand, hand in hand, they've ex - changed wed - ding bands. To -
find peace of mind comes, to all who are kind. May the
go, may they know ev - 'ry love that was shown. And as

E♭ B♭ C7 F7

day is the day___ of all their dreams and their plans,___ And
rough times a - head___ be - come___ tri - umphs in time.___
life it gets short - er, may___ their feel - ings grow.___ Wher -

B♭ B♭7 E♭ B♭

all of their loved ones are here to say.___
May___ their chil - dren be hap - py each day.___ Oh
ev - er they trav - el, wher - ev - er they stay,___ may

Eb
Bb
F7
Bb
God bless this coup - le who mar - ry to - day.
God bless this fam - 'ly who start - ed to - day.
God bless this coup - le who mar - ry to - day.

Chorus
F7
Eb
In good times and bad times, in sick - ness and

Bb
F7
C7
health, may they know that rich - es are not need - ed for

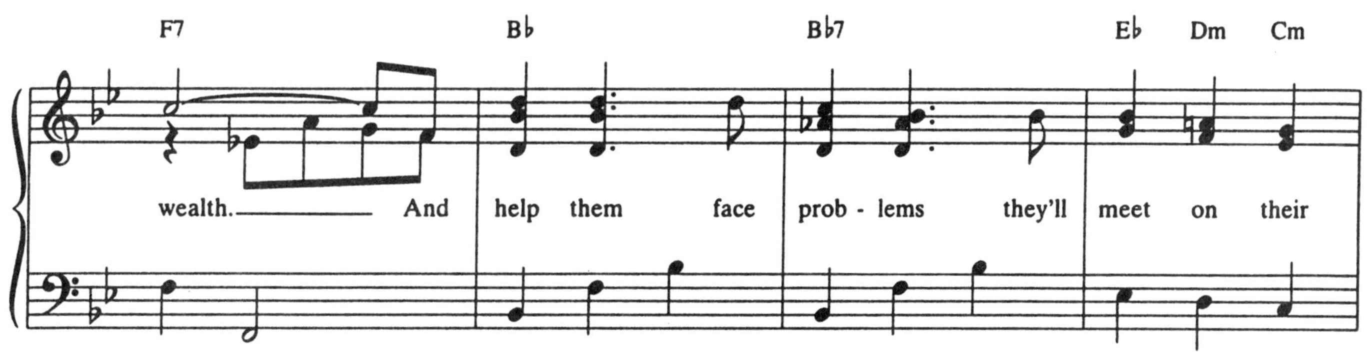
F7
Bb
Bb7
Eb
Dm
Cm
wealth. And help them face prob - lems they'll meet on their

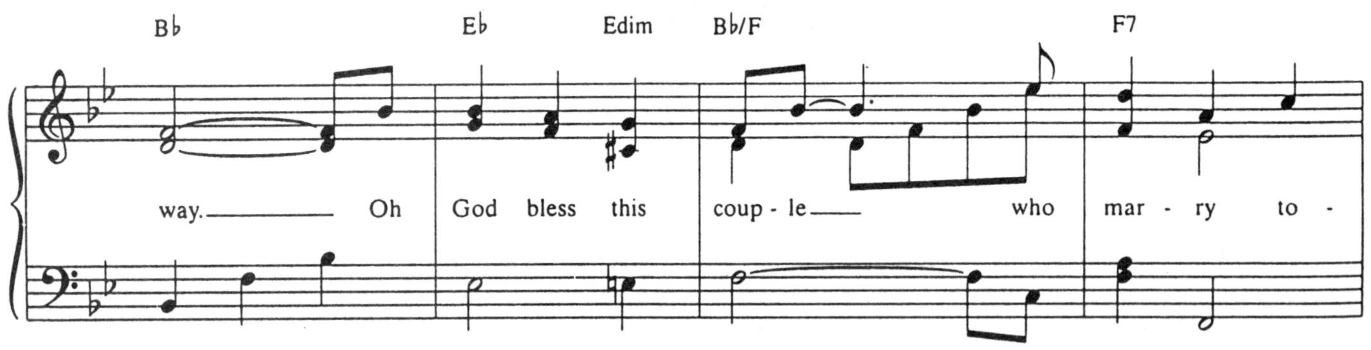
B♭
E♭
Edim
B♭/F
F7
way. Oh
God bless this
coup - le who
mar - ry to -

1., 2.
3.
B♭
D.C.
B♭
E♭
Edim
B♭/F
day.
day. Oh
God bless this
coup - le who

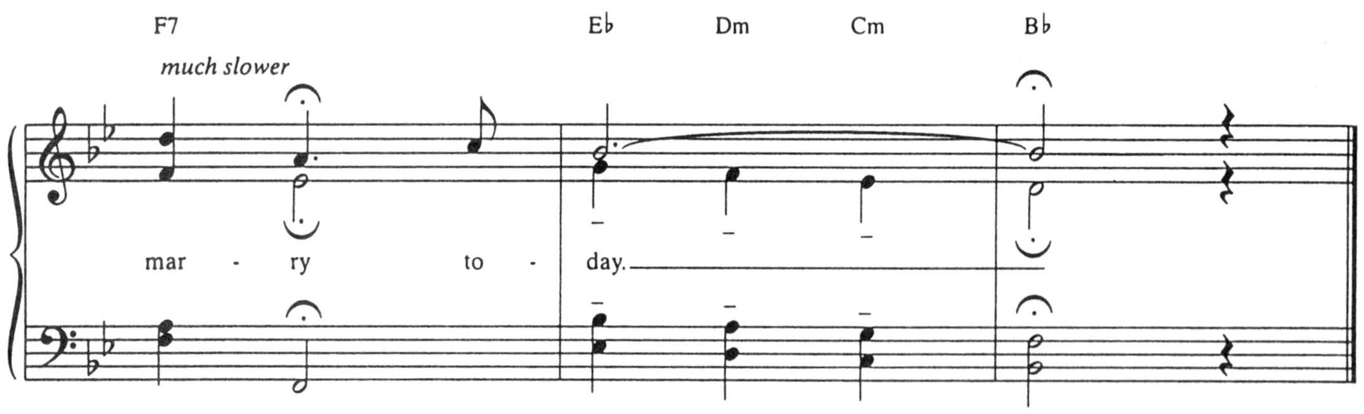
F7
much slower
E♭
Dm
Cm
B♭
mar - ry to -
day.

IT HAD TO BE YOU

Words by
GUS KAHN

Music by
ISHAM JONES

Em
A7
And e-ven be glad, just to be sad, thinking of you.

D7
Eb7-5
D7
D+
G
D+
G
Some oth-ers I've seen might nev-er be mean

E7
A7
Might nev-er be cross or try to be boss,

Em
but they would-n't do, for no-bod-y else
Am Am7 A°7 D7 G B7
gave me a thrill, with all your faults I love you still,
Em G°7 D7 G°7 D7
IT HAD TO BE YOU, won-der-ful you, HAD TO BE YOU.
1. G G°7 Cm6 D7 D+
2. G Cm6 G6
IT HAD TO BE YOU,

THE KEEPER OF THE STARS

Words and Music by
KAREN STALEY, DANNY MAYO
and DICKIE LEE

D
A/C♯
Bm
Now, I just can't be - lieve you're in my
I know I don't de - serve a trea - sure like
G
D/F♯
life. Heav-en's smil-in' down on me
you. There real - ly are no words
Em
A7sus
A
N.C.
D/F♯
as I look at you to - night.
to show my grat - i - tude.
I tip my
mf
Chorus:
G
A
F♯m
hat to the keep - er of the stars.

G
Em
A7
He sure knew what he___ was do - in'___ when he joined these two___

D
D/F♯
G
hearts. I hold ev - 'ry - thing

A
F♯m
G
D/F♯
Em
when I hold you in my___ arms. I've got all I'll ev-er need

1.
A
G
D
A7sus
thanks to the keep-er of___ the stars.___
dim.
mp

2.
A
D
thanks to the keep - er of___ the stars.__
dim.
A/C♯
Bm
mp
It was_ no ac - ci - dent,_ me find - ing
G
D/F♯
you.
Some-one had a hand_ in it___
Em
A7sus
D
A7sus
D
long be - fore_ we__ ev - er knew.
a tempo
dim. e rit.
p

LET'S PUT IT ALL TOGETHER

Words and Music by
HUGO & LUIGI, and
GEORGE DAVID WEISS

G
A/G
D/F#
Em7♭5
D/A
A7
Let's put it all to - geth - er, girl, 'Cause lov - in' is all there
1. D
G/D
D
2. G/D
D
G/D
D
G/D
D
Em/D
D
is.
is.
G/D
D
G/D
D
Em7
A7
D
Love like this nev - er hap - pened be - fore, per - fect and true,
G/D
D
G/D
D
E7sus4
E7
Day by day we been feel - in' it more, you love me and

A7sus4
A7
G
A/G
D/F#
Bm7
I love you. Let's put it all to - geth - er,
Em
A
D
Am7
D7
G
A/G
Let's put it all to - geth - er,
Let's put it all to -
D/F#
Em7♭5
D/A
A7
D
Am7
D7
geth - er, girl, 'Cause lov - in' is all there is.
Repeat and fade
G
A/G
D/F#
Bm7
Em
A
D
Am7
D7
Let's put it all to - geth- er,
Let's put it all to - geth- er.

LOVE OF MY LIFE

Words and Music by
BRIAN McKNIGHT

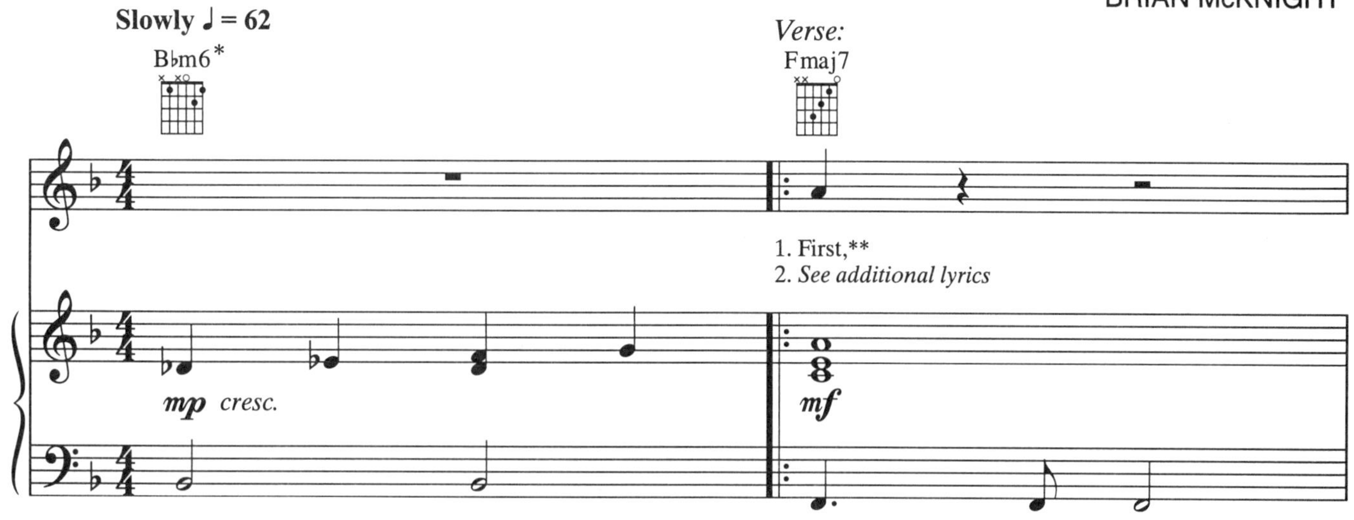

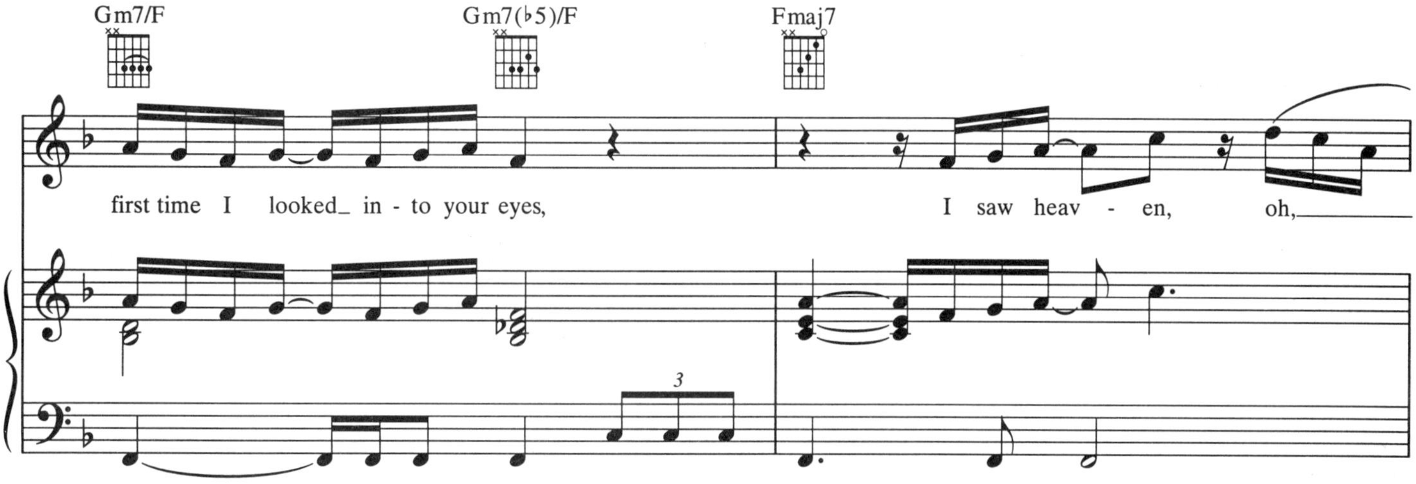

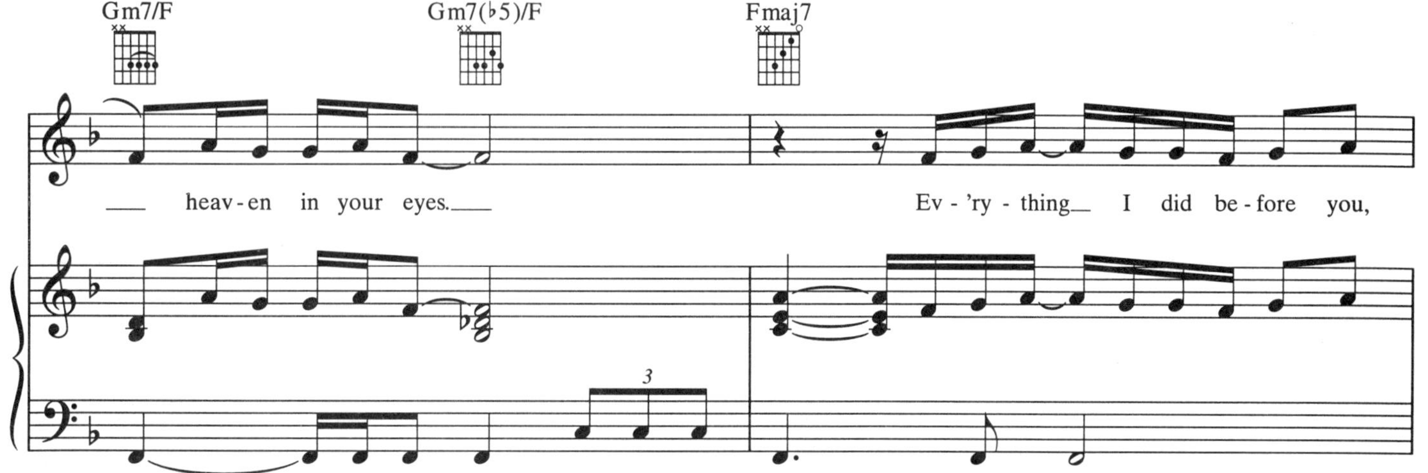

*Original recording in Gb major.
**Sung falsetto.

Gm7/F
Gm7(♭5)/F
Fmaj7
was - n't worth my while.
It should have been you, you
Gm7/F
Gm7(♭5)/F
D♭maj7(♯11)
C7sus
all the time.
I'll do an - y - thing and ev - 'ry - thing to please
Fmaj9
Dm7
Gm7
you.
You know how much I need you.
You're al - ways,
B♭m6
Chorus:
Fmaj7
al - ways on my mind.
You're more than won - der - ful,
more than a -

Gm7/F
Gm7(♭5)/F
Fmaj7
maz - ing, the ir - re - place - a - ble love of my
life. You're so in - cred - i - ble here in these arms to - night, the ir - re -
place - a - ble love of my life.
1.
2.
life.
Bridge:
Asus
A
A7(♭9)
Dm7
C/E
F
Ba - by, you know, you know you're my one and on - ly.

Dm7/G
G
C/E
B♭/D
All I wan - na do___ is be___ to - geth - er.______
A(9)/C♯
Dm7
C
Sug - ar, you know__ I'll nev - er leave you lone - ly.
G/B
B♭maj7
Gm7/C
Fmaj7
In your eyes, in your eyes, I see for - ev - er.
(vocal ad lib.)
Gm7/F
Gm7(♭5)/F
Fmaj7
1.
Gm7/F
Gm7(♭5)/F

Verse 2:
Always seems like a reality.
Forever don't seem so far away.
All I wanna do,
All I wanna feel,
All I wanna be
Is close to you.
Every day is my lucky day.
All I wanna do is love you.
I place no other above you.
I'll tell you why…
(To Chorus:)

LOST IN YOUR EYES

Words and Music by
DEBORAH ANN GIBSON

Am
F
F/G
C
Is it love that I am in?
F/G
G
C
F/C
I get weak in a glance. Is - n't
C
F/C
G/B
Am
this what's called ro - mance? And now I know 'cause when I'm
F
F/G
C
B♭/C
C
lost I can't let go.

F
F/G
C
I don't mind not know-ing what I'm head-ed for.
F
E7
Am
C7
You can take me to the skies.
F
G/F
Em
Am
Dm
Em
F
It's like be-ing lost in hea-ven when I'm lost in your
F/G
G
C
F/C
eyes. I just fell, don't know why. Some-thing's

C
F/C
G/B
Am
there we can't de-ny. And when I first knew was when
F
F/G
C
G/A
A
I first looked at you. And if
D
G/D
D
I can't find my way, if sal-va-tion seems worlds a
G/D
A/C♯
Bm
way, oh I'll be found when I am

Em
A
D
lost in your eyes.
Am/D
D
G
A
Oh woh.
I don't mind not know-ing what I'm
D
G
F#7
head-ed for.
You can take me to
Bm
D7
G
A/G
F#m
A#dim
Bm
the skies.
It's like be-ing lost in hea-ven when

Em
F♯m
G
Asus
A
D
I'm lost in your eyes. I get weak in a glance.
G/D
D
G/D
F♯7/C♯
Is - n't this what's called ro - mance? Oh, I'll be
Bm
Em
F♯m
Asus
found when I am lost in your
D
G/D
D(add9)
eyes. Oh.
rit.

LOVE LIKE OURS

Lyrics by
ALAN and MARILYN BERGMAN

Music by
DAVE GRUSIN

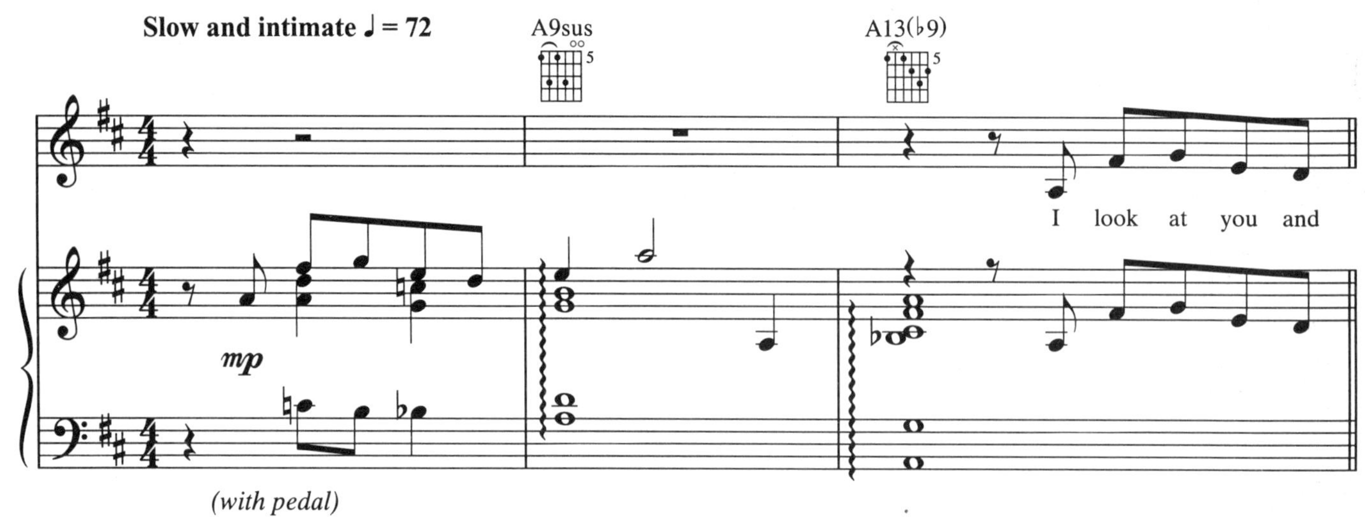

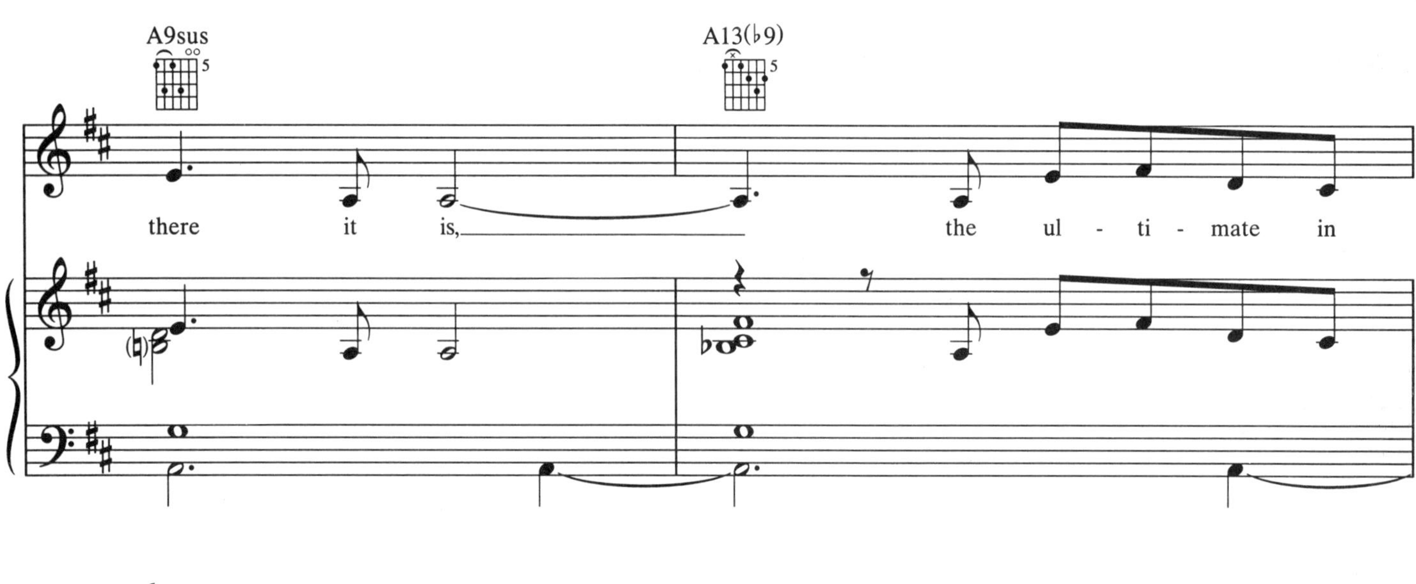

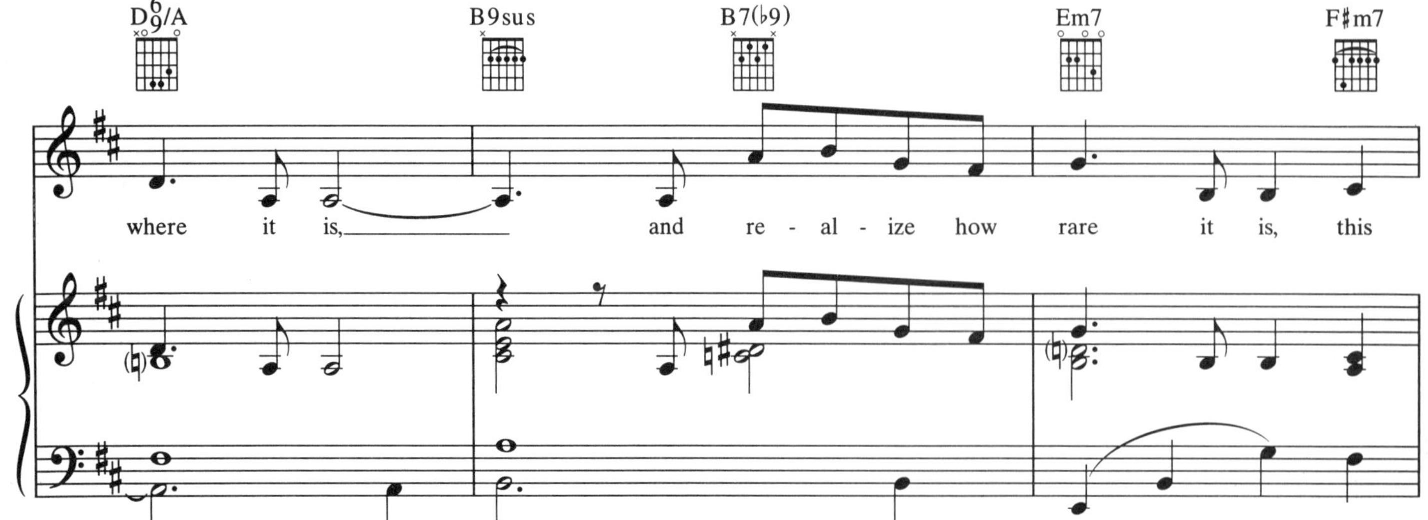

Gm/A A7(♭9) D A/C♯ F♯7

find - ing your love. You try so man - y

Bm9 E9sus C♯7/E♯

arms when you are lone - ly, to

F♯m9 B7sus(♭9) B7(♭9) C

find the one and on - ly. One day you

C9/B♭ A11 Dmaj9/A

turn and {she's / he's} there. A - maz - ing how se -

A9sus
Am11
A7(♭9)
Dmaj9/A
rene it is, the shade of ev - er - green it is,
B9sus
B7(♭9)
Em7
F♯m7
ex - act - ly what we mean it is, and
A11
A7(♭9)
D11
D7/C
knew it would be.
Bm9
Bm9/A
G♯m9
When love like ours ar - rives,

C♯11(♭9)
C♯7(♭9)
D(9)/C
B9sus
B7(♭9)
we guard it with our lives.
What - ev - er goes a -
Em7
F♯m7
A11
A7(♭9)/G
F♯13sus
F♯7(♯5 ♭9)
stray, what rain - y day comes a - round,
B9sus
B7sus(♭9)
C9/B♭
a love like ours will keep us
A11
A13(♭9)
D(9)
safe and sound.
rit.

MY EVERYTHING

Words and Music by
ARNTHOR BIRGISSON, ANDERS SVEN BAGGE,
NICK LACHEY and ANDREW LACHEY

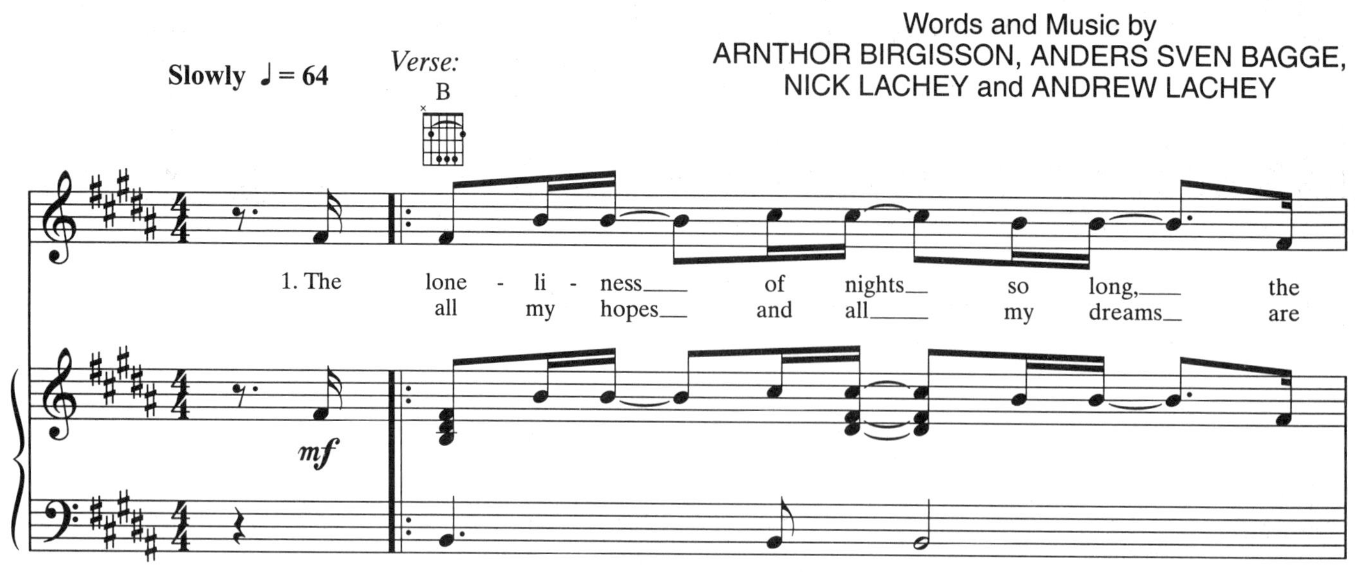

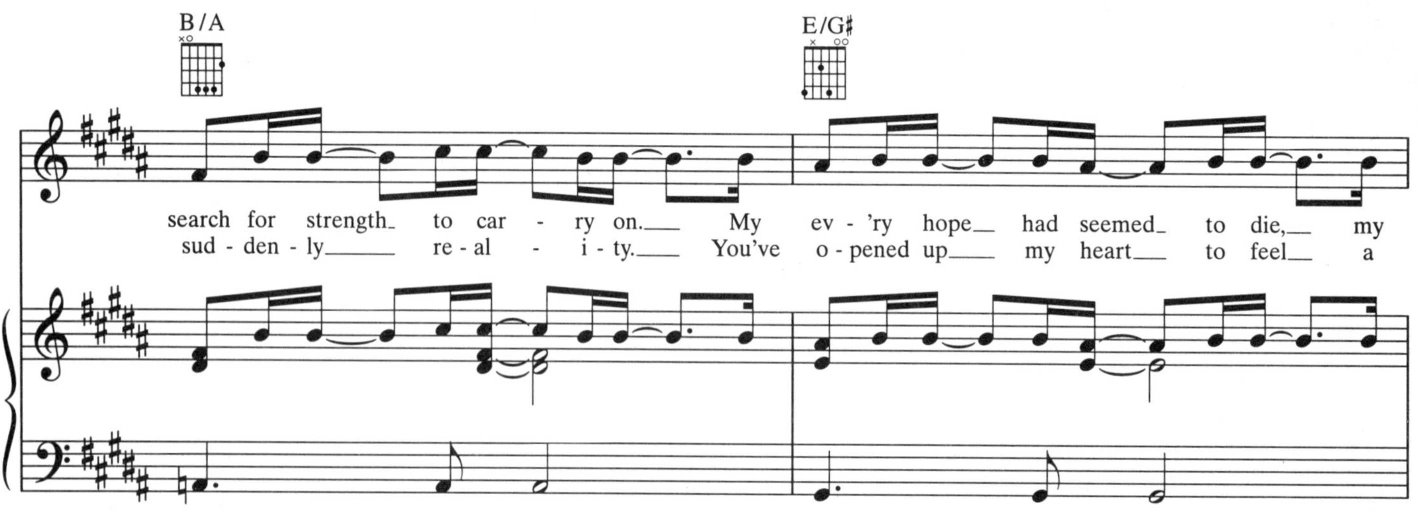

C♯/E♯
E
B/D♯
round - ed me___ with your end - less love.___ And all the things_ I could - n't see___ are
thing in life__ that I would ev - er trade._ For the love you give__ and won't_ let go,___ I
C♯m7
C♯m7/F♯
N.C.
Chorus:
B
F♯/A♯
now so clear to me.
hope you'll al - ways know...
You are my ev - 'ry - thing. Noth - ing your
G♯m7
G♯m7/F♯
E
love won't bring.___ My life is yours a - lone. The on - ly love I've
Em6/G
G♯m7
F♯
ev - er known.___ Your spir - it pulls me through when noth - ing

C♯7/E♯
C♯m7
else will do.
Ev - 'ry night I pray on bend - ed knee that
Amaj7
C♯m7/F♯
1.
B
you will al - ways be my ev - 'ry - thing.
2. Now
2.
B
B/A
Bridge:
Gmaj9
F♯m7
thing.
Oh,
you're the breath of life in me, the
F♯m7/B
B
B/A
Em9
Dmaj7
on - ly one that sets me free.
And you have made my soul com - plete for all

C♯m7
Dm7/G
N.C.
time, for all time. You are my
Chorus:
C
G/B
Am7
Am7/G
ev - 'ry - thing. Noth - ing your love won't bring. My life is
thing.
F
Fm6/A♭
yours a - lone. The on - ly love I've ev - er known. Your spir - it
Am7
G
D7/F♯
pulls me through when noth - ing else will do. Ev - 'ry

1.
Dm7
B♭maj7
Dm7/G
night I pray on bend - ed knee that you will al - ways be
You are my
my ev - e - ry -

2.
Dm7
Freely
B♭
Dm7/G
night I pray down on bend - ed knee that you will al - ways
rit.

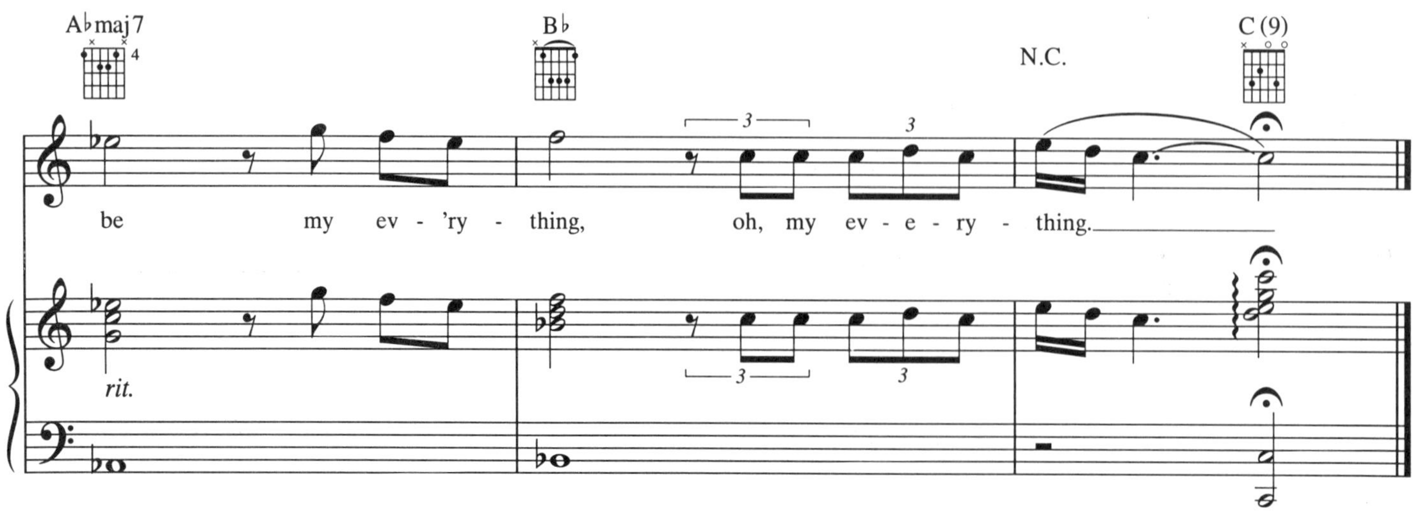
A♭maj7
B♭
N.C.
C (9)
be my ev - 'ry - thing, oh, my ev - e - ry - thing.
rit.

ONE HEART ONE LOVE

Words and Music by
GARY BROWN and BARRY EASTMOND

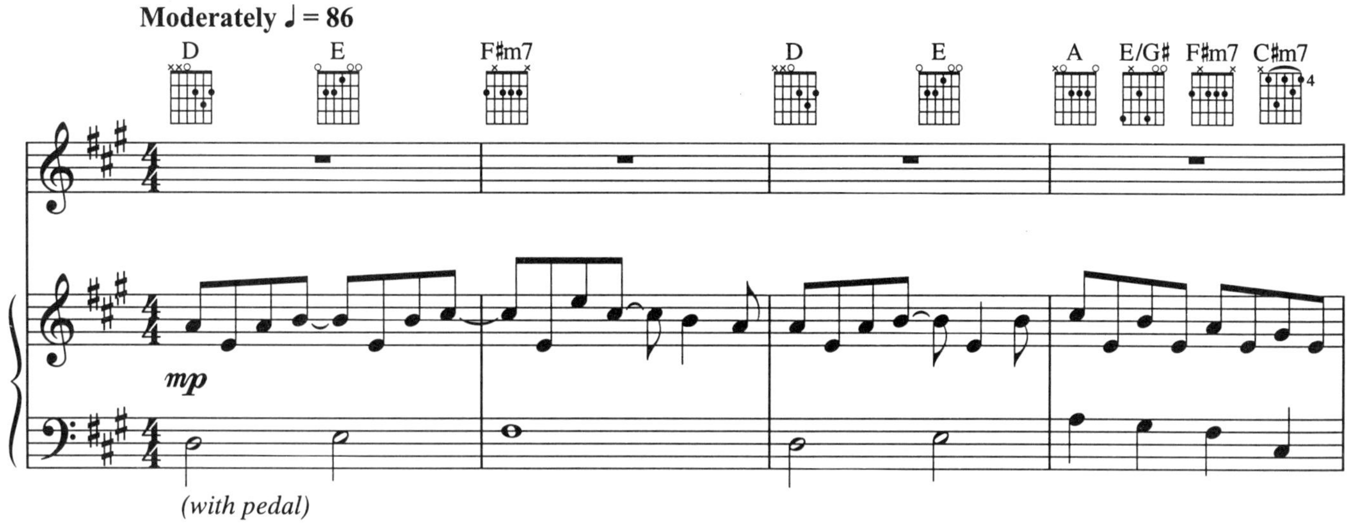

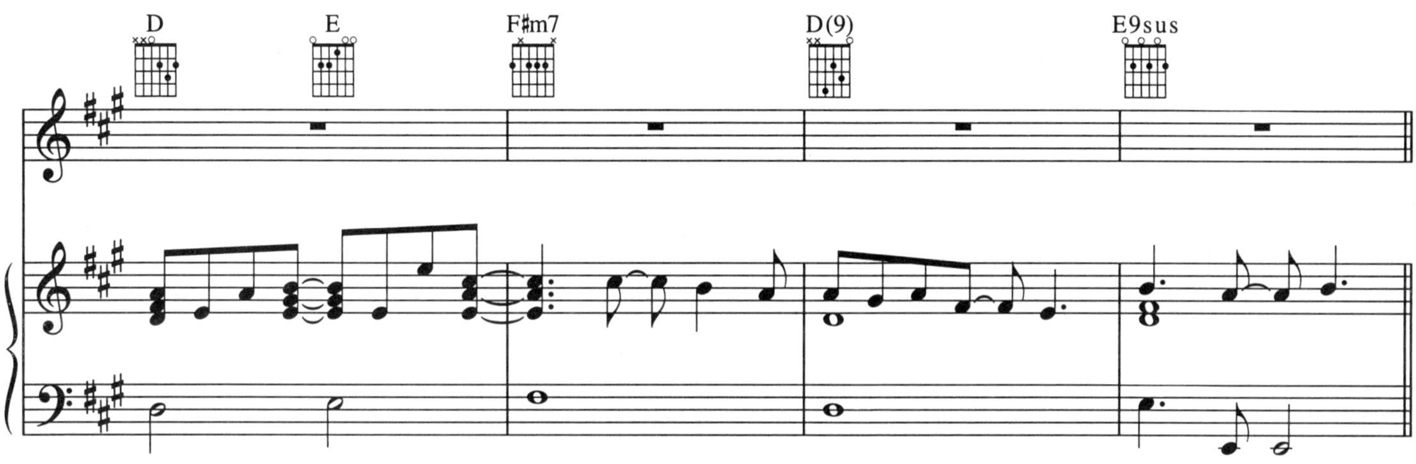

D
E
A
E/G♯
F♯m7
C♯m7
What bet - ter way to show my faith in you. Giv - in' you the lock and the
You o - pened up and gave your love to me. And I'll be yours for all
key. In oth - er words, ba - by, give you all of me. 'Cause
time, twen - ty - four sev - en, both day and night.
D(9)
Bm7
C♯
I've searched this world a - round and 'round for
I've searched this world from moun - tain high to
some - one like you. And I thank my stars
riv - er deep. And now that you're here,

C#
D(9)
E
I fi - n'lly found a wom-an like you.
I'm yours for life, I'm yours to keep.
Chorus:
D
E
F#m7
D
E
One heart, one love, one love now, ba - by. I'm giv-ing my all for you,
A
E/G#
F#m7
C#m7
D
E
A
sweet ba - by. One heart, one love. For the
D(9)
1.
E9sus
2.
E9sus
rest of my days I prom-ise that I'll be true. prom-ise that I'll be true.

Bridge:
G
D/F♯
A
One love for the rest of my life, that's all I want, ba - by,
that's all I need, ba - by. One heart that beats for all time
G
D/F♯
E7sus
Bm7
C♯m7
for you, for you. I don't need mon - ey,
Dm7
Dm7/G
Cm7
F9sus
for-tune or fame. What I need, my love, is for you to share my name.

Chorus:
E♭
F
Gm7
E♭
F
One heart, one love, one love now, ba - by. I'm giv-ing my all to you
B♭
F/A
Gm7
Dm7
E♭
F
B♭
now, ba - by. One heart, one love. For the
E♭(9)
1.
F9sus
rest of my days I prom - ise that I'll be true.
2.
F9sus
Cm7
F
B♭
prom-ise that I'll be true to you.

MY OWN TRUE LOVE

Based on "Tara Theme"

Words by
MACK DAVID

Music by
MAX STEINER

MY OWN TRUE LOVE, No lips but yours, No arms but yours
Will ev - er lead me through heav-en's doors; I roamed the earth
In search of this, I knew I'd know you, know you
by your kiss, And by your kiss You've shown true love, I'm yours for-
ev - er, MY OWN TRUE LOVE. LOVE.
mp
col 8

ONCE IN A LIFETIME

Words and Music by
WALTER AFANASIEFF, MICHAEL BOLTON
and DIANE WARREN

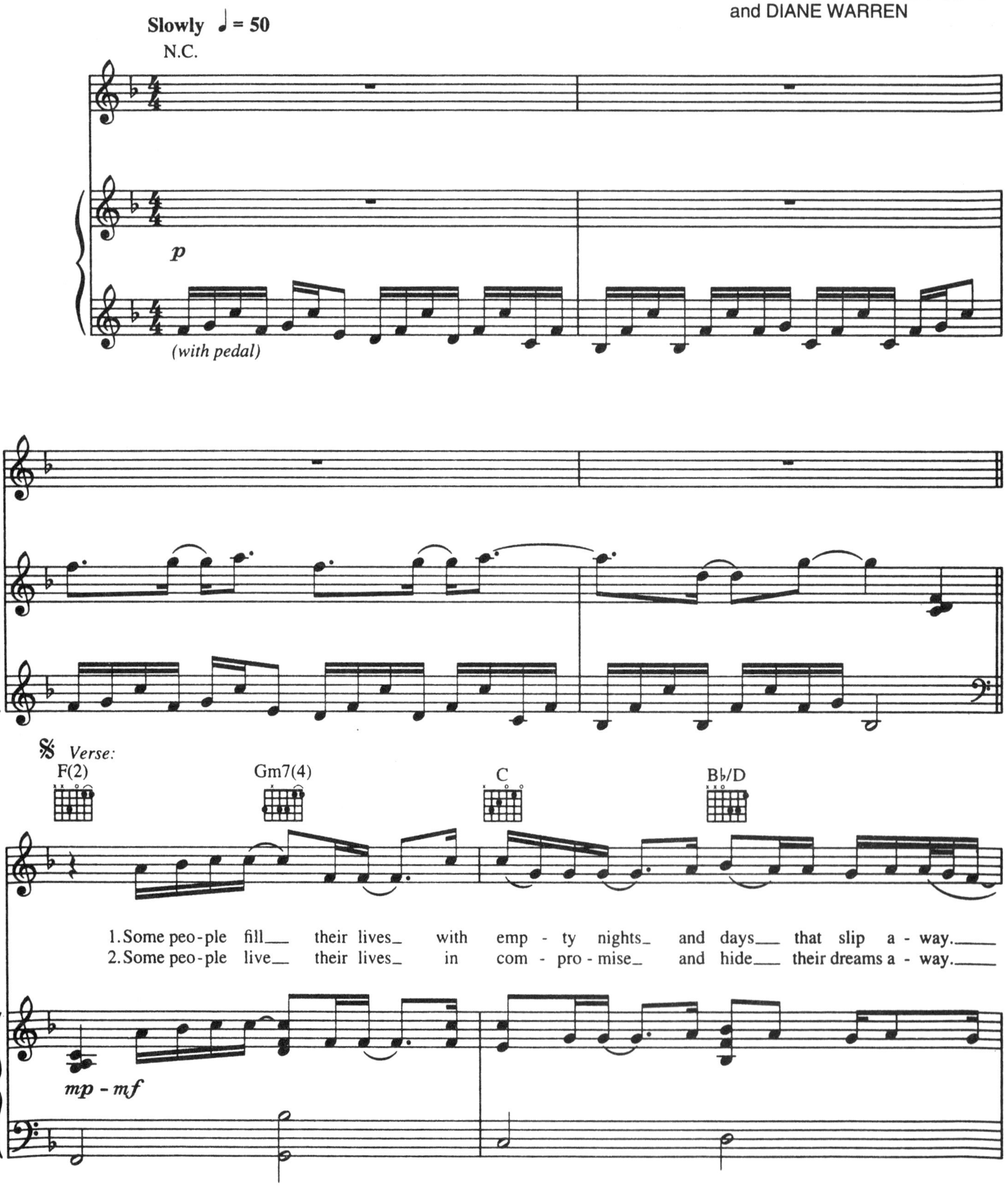

𝄋 *Verse:*

F(2) Gm7(4) C B♭/D

1. Some peo-ple fill__ their lives_ with emp - ty nights_ and days__ that slip a - way.____
2. Some peo-ple live__ their lives_ in com - pro - mise_ and hide__ their dreams a - way.____

mp - mf

Dm
Gm7
C
A7/C♯
Some search till the end of time, but nev - er find the o - pen arms of fate.
Some nev - er take the chance with - in their hands to claim the prize they make.
Dm
Fmaj7/C
Bm7(♭5)
N.C.
One mo - ment comes a - long, and some-one hands your
When faith is all you need to hold the hand of
B♭6
B♭m(maj7)
Gm7/C
C7
dreams to you, and all at once your dreams come true.
des - ti - ny, and find the love that's meant to be.
Once in a life -
Chorus:
F
C/E
Dm
B♭/D
C7/E
F
- time, you find the one you real - ly love, for

Dm
F/A
Gm7
C7sus
now and for - ev - er, one love that nev - er ends. Once in a life-
F
C/E
Dm
B♭/D
C7/E
A7/C♯
Dm
- time, when ev-'ry star that lights the sky will
F/A
B♭(2)
Gm7(4)
Gm7
B♭/C
shine with one rea - son, lead-ing your heart to the one love you find just once in a
1.
F
C/E
Dm7
B♭(2)
C7sus
D.S. 𝄋
life - time.

2.
F
Db
Eb/Db
life - time.
If you be - lieve in the pow - er of love,
cresc.
f
Ab/C
Gb/Bb
Ab/C
Db
Ab/C
then you be - lieve that dreams come true.
Mag - ic will fill your heart when that
Bbm7
Db/Eb
F/A
Bb(2)
mo - ment comes a - long just once in your life.
F/C
A/C#
Dm
F/A
Bb(2)
C7sus
N.C.
Once in a

Gb
Db/F
Ebm
Cb/Db
Db/F
Gb
life-time,
you find the one you real - ly love,
for
Ebm
Gb/Bb
Abm7
Db7sus
now and for-ev - er, one love that nev - er ends.
Once in a life-
Gb
Db/F
Ebm
Fm7(b5)
Bb7
Ebm
- time,
when ev-'ry star that lights the sky
will
Cb
Gb/Bb
Abm7(4)
Abm7
Cb/Db
shine with one rea - son, lead-ing you home to the one love you'll find just once in a

Gb Db/F Ebm7 Cb(2) Dbsus

life - time. Just once in a life -

mp

Gb Db/F Ebm7 Cb(2) Dbsus

- time.___ Once in a life -

Gb(2) Ebm7 Gb/Bb Cb(2) Dbsus

- time._ *(2nd time, begin ad lib. vocals)* Once in a life-

Gb(2) Ebm7 Gb/Bb Cb(2)

Repeat ad lib. and fade

- time._ Once in a life -

THE SEARCH IS OVER

Words and Music by
JIM PETERIK and FRANK SULLIVAN

Ab
4 fr.
Gsus4
G7/B
Cm
3 fr.
doubt - ing what you feel?
I was al - ways
ques - tions of the heart.
You fol - lowed me through
des - ti - nies are one.
So if you ev - er
Bb/C
Abmaj7
4 fr.
Eb
Bb/D
reach - ing.
You were just a girl I
chang - es and pa - tient - ly you'd wait till
loved me show me that you give a
Cm
3 fr.
Gm7
3 fr.
Ab
4 fr.
Gsus4
knew. I took for grant - ed the friend I have in you.
I came to my sen - ses through some mir - a - cle of fate.
damn. You'll know for cer - tain the man I real - ly am.

G7
F/G
G7
C
G/B
F/A
Gsus4
I was liv - ing for a dream, lov - ing for a mo - ment.
Tak - ing on the world, that was just my style.
Eb
Abmaj7
4 fr.
Now I look in - to your eyes I can see for - ev - er.
Now I look in - to your eyes I can see for - ev - er.
Then I touched your hand I could hear you whis - per.
Fm7
B°7
Cm
3 fr.
To Coda
Ab
Bb7
The search is o - ver, you were with me all the
you were
love was

1.
Eb
2.
Eb
Bb/D
while.
while.
Now the
Cm
3 fr.
Gm7
3 fr.
Ab
4 fr.
Bb7
miles stretch out be - hind __ me, loves that I __ have
Eb
Bb/D
Cm
3 fr.
Gm7
3 fr.
Ab
4 fr.
Bb/Ab
lost. Bro-ken hearts lie vic - tims of the dead.
Ab
4 fr.
Fm7
Cm
3 fr.
Then girl, like, it fi - n'lly struck __ like

Bb
Fm7
light - nin' from the blue;
ev - er - y high - way is
Eb
Bb
D. S. al Coda
lead - in' me back to you.
Coda
Ab
4 fr.
Bb7
Eb
Ab/Eb
4 fr.
Bb/Eb
Eb
right be - fore my eyes.
rit.
a tempo
Ab/Eb
4 fr.
Bb/Eb
Eb
Ab
4 fr.
Bb
Eb
rit.

THIS I PROMISE YOU

Words and Music by
RICHARD MARX

Asus
A
A2
Bm7
fore.
and all that sur - rounds you
And I prom - ise you, nev - er
G(9)
Asus
A
Em7
are se - crets and lies,
I'll be your strength,
will you hurt an - y - more.
I give you my word. I
A7
D
A/C♯
Bm7
I'll give you hope,
keep - ing your faith when it's gone.
The
give you my heart.
This is a bat - tle we've won.
And
omit 2nd time
Em7
Gm6
Asus
one you should call
was stand - ing here all a - long.
with this vow,
for - ev - er has now be - gun.

𝄋 *Chorus:*

Asus A D A

And I will take you in my arms and
Just close your eyes each lov - ing day and
3. *(Inst. solo ad lib.…*

Bm7 G D/A *To Coda* 𝄌

hold you right where you be - long.
know this feel - ing won't go a - way.
'Til the day my life is

A Gmaj9 1. D

through, this I prom - ise you. This I prom - ise you.

2. D *Bridge:* Em7 A

ise you. O-ver and o-ver I fall

Em7
A
D
A
G
when I hear you call. With-out you in my life,
D.S. 𝄋 al Coda
Em7
Asus
A
baby, I just would-n't be liv - ing at all.
Coda
Chorus:
A
N.C.
E
B
...end solo) And I will take you in my arms and
close your eyes each lov - ing day and
C♯m7
A
E/B
hold you right where you be - long. 'Til the day my life is
know this feel - ing won't go a - way. Ev - 'ry word I say is

1. 2.

B A B

through, this I prom - ise you. Just through, this I prom -

Amaj9 E

ise you. Ev - 'ry word I say is

B Amaj9

true, this I prom - ise you. Ooh, I prom -

E A/E E A/E E

ise you.

rit.

SO IN LOVE WITH YOU

Words and Music by
LINDA THOMPSON, DAVID FOSTER
and BILL ROSS

F/C
B♭/C
C7
F
I'm not a-shamed to say___ that I feel this way.___ I will
Chorus:
B♭maj7
C
Am7
C/D
D7
Gm7
Gm7/C
C7
stand be - fore God,_ give you all that I've got,_ I can prom - ise you_ I'll be true._
mf
F
Gm7
Am7
B♭maj7
C
1.
Am7
C/D
D7
___ I re - veal here and now_ as we both take this vow,_
Gm7
Gm7/C
C7(♭9)
F
C7
B♭/D
C7/E
I am so_ in love with you.
mp
dim.

2.
Am7 C/D D7 Gm7 Gm7/C C7(♭9)
both take this vow,
I am so in love,
I am so in love with
dim.
mp
F F/E B♭/D B♭m/D♭ F/C B♭maj7 Am7 F F/E
you.
(Spoken:) I promise to honor and cherish you for better or for worse, I'll be there for you. For richer or for poorer,
f
mp
B♭/D B♭m/D♭ F/C B♭maj7 Am7 Am7/D Gm7 B♭ C B♭/C C D
in sickness and in health, till death do us part,
from this day on and forever.
I will
f
Cmaj7 D Bm7 D/E E7 Am7 Am7/D D7
stand be - fore God,
give you all that I've got,
I can prom - ise you
I'll be true.

G Am7 Bm7 Cmaj7 D Bm7 Am/E E7

I re - veal here and now as we both take this vow,

Am7 Am7/D D7(♭9) Am7 Am7/D D7(♭9)

I am so in love, I am so in love, I am so in love with

dim.

G G/F♯ C/E G/D Cmaj7 Bm7 Am7 Am7/D G

you. I am so in love with you.

mp *rit.*

Verse 2:
Words can't express what I confess with each beat of my heart,
I'm overwhelmed with the passion I felt from the start.
Our love will grow as the years come and go
I'll remain by your side, oh yes I will.
There isn't anything that I would deny.
(To Chorus:)

THIS IS THE NIGHT

Words and Music by
CHRISTOPHER BRAIDE, GARY BURR
and ALDO NOVA

G♯m
A
Bsus
B
ev - 'ry kiss is a kiss you can nev - er get back. Lift me
Chorus:
E
F♯m7
E/G♯
A(9)
C♯m
C♯m/B
Amaj9
up, in your eyes. If you
E
F♯m7
E/G♯
A2
D
A/C♯
told me that is what heav - en is, well, you'd be right.
B
C♯m7
E/B
A2
Bsus
I've been wait - ing for - ev - er for this. This is the

Verse 2:
E5
C♯m
D
E
night. 2. When the an - swer to all my dreams is as
C♯m
D
E
G♯m
close as a touch a - way, why am I here, hold - ing back
A(9)
Bsus
B
what I'm try - ing to say? Lift me
Chorus:
E
F♯m7
E/G♯
A(9)
C♯m
C♯m/B
Amaj9
up, in your eyes. If you

E
F♯m7
E/G♯
A(9)
Bsus
B
told me that is what heav - en is, well, you'd be right.
Hold me
E
F♯m7
E/G♯
A(9)
C♯m
C♯m/B
Amaj9
close
to your heart.
I would
E
F♯m7
E/G♯
A(9)
D
go with you to the ends of the earth and we'll fly.
Bsus
B
C♯m7
E/B
A
Bsus
E
B/D♯
I've been wait-ing for-ev - er for this.
This is the night.

Bridge:
C♯m
A
E
B
This is the night_ where we cap - ture for - ev - er and all___ our to - mor - rows be - gin.___
C♯m
A
B
Af - ter to - night_ we will nev - er be lone - ly a - gain.___ Lift me
Chorus:
E
F♯m7
E/G♯
A(9)
C♯m
C♯m/B
Amaj9
up,___ in your eyes.___ If you
E
F♯m7
E/G♯
A(9)
Bsus
B
C♯
told me that_ is what heav - en is, well,_ you'd be right.___ Hold me

F♯ G♯m7 F♯/A♯ B(9) D♯m7 F♯/C♯ Bmaj9

close ___ to your heart. ___ I would

F♯ G♯m7 F♯/A♯ B(9) E

go with you_ to the ends_ of the earth_ and we'll fly. ___

C♯sus C♯ D♯m7 F♯/C♯ B(9)

___ I've been wait - ing for - ev - er for this. ___

rit.

C♯sus F♯ G♯m7 F♯/A♯ B F♯(9)

This is the_ night. ___

a tempo *rit.*

TONIGHT I CELEBRATE MY LOVE

Words and Music by
MICHAEL MASSER and GERRY GOFFIN

Eb
Cm7
Fm7
Ab/Bb
Ab
night no one's gon - na find us, we'll leave the world be -
night our spir - its will be climb - ing to a sky lit up with
mf
Gm7
Cm9
1. Fm7
Ab/Bb
hind us, when I make love to you. 2. To -
dia - monds when I make
mp
2. Abmaj7
Ab/Bb
Eb
Bb/Eb
love to you to - night.
Ab/Eb
To next strain
3. Abmaj7
Ab/Bb
Bb
To - love to you. To -

Chorus:
A♭maj7
Gm7
D♭/E♭
E♭7
night I cel - e - brate my love for you and the
f
mid - night sun is gon - na come shin - ing through. To -
Fm7
Cm7
night there'll be no dis - tance be - tween us. What I want
A♭m(♯7)
most to do is to get close to you to -
decresc.

Verse 3:
Tonight I celebrate my love for you,
And soon this old world will seem brand new.
Tonight we will both discover
How friends turn into lovers,
When I make love to you.
(To Chorus:)

AND I LOVE YOU SO

Words and Music by
DON McLEAN

Am Dm7 F

But life be-gan a-gain, The day you took my
All but love is dead, That is my be-

C

hand.
lief.
And, yes, I know how

Dm7 G7 G7♭9

lone-ly life can be, The shad-ows fol-low me and the
(love-less)

C F C F Cmaj7 Am

night won't set me free. But I don't let the

Dm7
eve - ning get me down,
(bring)
Now that you're a -
G7
G7♭9
C
C6
round
me.
me.
D.S. al Coda
CODA
F
G7
I tell them
I don't
Dm
Fm
know.
rit.

WEDDING SONG

(There Is Love)

E
F♯7/E bass
there is love.
oh there's love.
A (add B)
E bass
E
Fine
Well, a
E
B/F♯ bass
A (add B)
E
man shall leave his mother and a woman leave her home,
C♯m
4 fr.
E
B/F♯ bass
they shall travel on to where the two shall be as one.
As it
E
B/F♯ bass
A (add B)
E
was in the beginning is now and 'til the end,
loving is the answer, then who's the giving for?
Do
C♯m
4 fr.
E
B/F♯ bass
woman draws her life from man and gives it back again and there is
you believe in something that you've never seen before?
Oh, there's

A (add B)
love, ___
love, ___
there is
oh, there's
1.
E
F♯7/E bass
love.
A/E bass
E
Well, then
A
A/G♯ bass
F♯m
B
E
what's to be the rea - son for be - com-ing man and wife? Is it
A
A/G♯ bass
F♯m
B
E
love that brings you here, or love that brings you life? For if
2.
E
D. S. 𝄋 al fine
love.
Oh, the

WHAT ARE YOU DOING THE REST OF YOUR LIFE?
Lyrics by ALAN and MARILYN BERGMAN
Music by MICHEL LEGRAND
Moderately, with feeling
mp
Am
Am (G♯ bass)
Am (G bass)
Am (F♯ bass)
What Are You Do - ing The Rest Of Your Life? North and south and east and
mf legato
Fmaj7
Dm7
west of your life? I have on - ly one re - quest of your life:
Bm7-5
Bm7 (E bass)
E7
Am
Am (G♯ bass)
that you spend it all with me: All the sea-sons and the times of your days,

Am (G bass)
Am (F# bass)
Fmaj7
All the nick-els and the dimes of your days. Let the rea-sons and the
Dm7
Bm7-5
E7
Amaj7
A
rhymes of your days all be-gin and end with me. I want to
Bm7-5
E9
Amaj7
Bm7-5
E9
see your face in ev-'ry kind of light. In fields of dawn and for-ests of the
Amaj7
Abm7
Db7-9
Gbmaj7
night. And when you stand be-fore the can-dles on a cake, Oh, let me be the
Gm7
C7-9
Fmaj9
Am
Am (G# bass)
one to hear the si-lent wish you make! Those to-mor-rows wait-ing deep in your eyes,

Am (G bass)
Am (F♯ bass)
Fmaj7
In the world of love you keep in your eyes, I'll a - wak - en what's a -
Dm7
Bm7-5
Bm7 (E bass)
E7
sleep in your eyes. It may take a kiss or two! Thru
cresc.
F6
Bm7-5
E9
Fmaj7
all of my life, Sum - mer, win - ter, spring and fall of my life,
F7-5
Am (E bass)
Bm7
E7+5
E7
All I ev - er will re - call of my life is all of my life with
1 Am
Bm7-5
E7
2. Am
Ddim
Am
Ddim
Am
you! What Are You Do - ing The you!
decresc.
rit. e dim.

WHEN I FALL IN LOVE

Words by
EDWARD HEYMAN

Music by
VICTOR YOUNG

A9sus
A7(♭9)
Dm
Gm6/D
gun and too man - y moon - light kiss - es seem to
Dm
G6/B
F/G
Slowly ♩. = 63
C
Fm/C
C
cool in the warmth of the sun.
Female: When I give my
Fm/C
C
Fm6/C
C7(♭9)
heart it will be com -
D7/C
G7(♭9)
C
Dm7
Em7
Fmaj9
Gm7/A
A7(♯5)
- plete - ly, or I'll nev - er give my

C/D
D13
Fmaj7/G
G13(♯11 ♭9)
heart. M: Don't let me give my heart. F: And the
Cmaj9
Am7
F♯m11
B7(♯11 ♭9)
D/E
Em11
A7(♭5)
A7
mo - ment I can feel that you feel that way
Dm9
B♭9
C/G
Fm6/G
Gdim7
too, M: I feel that way too, F: is when I fall in
D7/G
G7(♭9)
C
G/A
love, M: I'll fall in love Both: with you.

Dm9
Fm
C/D
G7sus
C
Fm/C
C
Both: When I fall in love
Fm6/C
C
B♭13
A13
it will be for - ev - er,
D9
G9sus
G7(♭9)
C
Dm7
Em7
Fmaj9
or I'll nev - er fall
Gm7/A
A7(♭9)
C/D
D13
F: in love.
M: Oh, I'll nev - er, nev - er fall

Fmaj7/G
G7(♭9)
Cmaj7
Am7
in love. Both: In a rest - less world like
B♭9(♯11)
C
Gm/B♭
Em7(♭5)/A
A7(♭9)
this is, love is end - ed be - fore it's be - gun, and too
Dm7
A7/D
man - y moon - light kiss - es seem to
Dm
A9sus
cool in the warmth of the sun.

D
Gm/D
D
Gm/D
When I give my heart
D
C9
B7(♭9)
Em7
Em7/A
A7
it will be com - plete - ly,
D
Em7
F♯m9
Gmaj9
Am7/B
B7(♭9)
F: or I'll nev - er give,
my heart,
M: I'll nev - er give,
E13sus
E13
Em7/A
A7(♯11 ♭9)
Both: And the
oh, I'll nev - er give my heart.

Dmaj7 Bm7 A/G C♯7(♭9 ♭5)

mo - ment___ I can feel______ that___ you___

Freely

F♯m7 B7(♭9) Em7 C9

___ feel___ that___ way___ too______________ *M:* is

D/A Gm6/A D7(♭9)/A E7/A Gm6/A F/C B♭m6/C F7(♭9)/C G7/C B♭m6/C

when I fall in love, *F:* when I fall in love,

D/A Gm6/A D7(♭9)/A Bm6/A A7 D E/D Gm6/D D

Both: when I fall in love with you.______________

molto rit.

WITH THIS RING

Words and Music by
KENNY LOGGINS and RICHARD MARX

Slowly ♩ = 56

G Em9 Gmaj7/B

mf

(with pedal)

Cmaj9 G Em9

Gmaj7/B Cmaj9

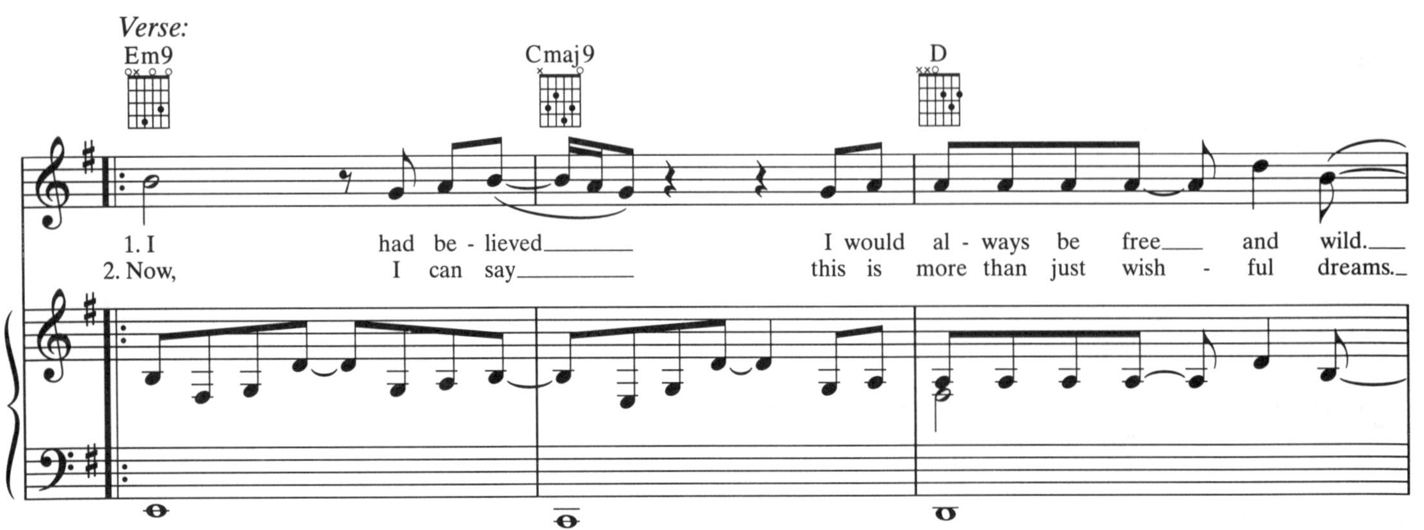

G G/F♯ Cmaj9 G/D D
No prom - is - es made or bro - ken. But
But noth - ing could be more real than
Em9 Cmaj9 D
look at me now, I come to you like a child,
love has a way of bring - ing you to your knees,
G G/F♯ Cmaj9 G/D D
here with my arms wide o - pen. I
lift - ing you up to heav - en. I see the
B7sus B7 Em Em/D
fol - low the sound that the voice in - side whis - pers to my soul.
rest of my life when I look in your eyes. I love what I see,

A(9)/C♯
Am7
Gmaj7/B
How could I not? It's my heart that brought me to par-
liv - ing with you on the sun - rise side of par-
Cmaj9
Chorus:
G(9)
a - dise.
a - dise.
I'll be your lov - er, I'll be your friend.
Em9
Cmaj9
Am7
I'll be the sum - mer breeze that nev - er ends. For the rest of your days,
Em9
Bm7
A(9)/C♯
I'll be the road that takes you home.

B/D♯
Em
Em(maj7)
Like the sun___ and the moon and the star_____ that guides_ you___ on,__
Em7
G7/C
Cm6
G(9)
__ I will___ be true. to my heart. I prom - ise you
C
D
1.
G
Em9
with this ring.
Bm7
Cmaj9
2.
G
C/G
ring.

Bridge:
G
Am9
Em9
May this___ cir - cle___ nev -
Cmaj7
D
G
Bm7
er see___ an___ end.___ Here and___ now,_
A(9)/C♯
Dm9
___ I will - ing - ly place___ a part___ of you___ up - on___ my___
Chorus:
Esus
E
A(9)
hand. I'll be your lov - er, I'll be your friend._

F♯m9
Dmaj9
I'll be the sum - mer breeze that nev -
Bm7
F♯m9
er ends. For the rest of your days,
I'll be the road
C♯m7
B(9)/D♯
that takes you home.
C♯/E♯
F♯m
Just like the sun and the moon and the star

F♯m(maj7)
F♯m7
Dm(maj7)
that guides you on, I will be true
Dm6
A(9)
D
E
to my heart. I prom-ise you with this
F♯m7
C♯m7
D2
ring. Oh,
Dm(maj7)
Dm6
A(9)
with this ring.

YOU'RE THE INSPIRATION

Words and Music by
DAVID FOSTER and
PETER CETERA

Eb
E
F/A
F#/A#
Bb
B
Eb/G
E/G#
Ab(add 2)
Aadd2
— of time. You — should know — eve - ry - where I go; —
D/F#
Eb/G
Gm
G#m
C/E
C#/E#
F
F#
D/F#
Eb/G
G
Ab
A/C#
Bb/D
al - ways on — my mind, — in my heart, — in my soul, — ba - by.
cresc.
Chorus:
D
Eb
D/F#
Eb/G
G
Ab
D/A
Eb/Bb
A
Bb
You're the mean - ing of my life, — you're the in - spi - ra - tion.
f
You bring feel - ing to my life, — you're the in - spi - ra - tion.

F
C/F
Bb/F
Bbm/F
Gb
Db/Gb
Cb/Gb
Cbm/Gb
Wan-na have you near me, I wan-na have you near me say - ing
1.
F/C
Bb/C
C
Fno3rd/Eb
Fno3rd
Gb/Db
Cb/Db
Db
F#no3rd/E
F#no3rd
no one needs you more than I need you.
Bb
Eb
F
B
E
F#
D.S.
2.
F/C
Bb/C
C9
Gb/Db
Cb/Db
Db9
2. And I no one needs you more than
mp
f
mp
Bb/C
A/C#
D
D/F#
G
D/A
A
Cb/Db
Bb/D
Eb
Eb/G
Ab
Eb/Bb
Bb
I need you.
(no one needs you more than I.)

D
Eb
D/F#
Eb/G
G
Ab
D/A
Eb/Bb
A
Bb
F
Gb
C/F
Db/G
Wan-na have you near me, I
Bb/F
Cb/Gb
Bbm/F
Cbm/Gb
F/C
Gb/Db
Bb/C
Cb/Db
wan-na have you hear me say yeah, no one needs you more than I
C
Db
A/C#
Bb/D
E
F
E/G#
F/A
need you. You're the mean-ing of my life,
A
Bb
E/B
F/C
B
C
E
F
C#m
Dm
F#m9
Gm9
you're the in-spi-ra-tion. you bring feel-ing to my life, you're the in-spi-ra-tion. When you

𝄋 *Verse 2:*
And I know (yes, I know)
That it's plain to see
We're so in love when we're together.
Now I know (now I know)
That I need you here with me
From tonight until the end of time.
You should know everywhere I go;
Always on my mind, you're in my heart, in my soul.

(To Chorus:)

CONGA

Words and Music by
ENRIQUE GARCIA

Chorus:

Em D Em D D Em D Em Em

Come ___ on, shake your bod - y, ba - by, do the con - ga. (I) know ___ you can't con-trol your - self an-y long - er. Feel ___ the rhy-thm of the mu-sic get-ting strong - er. Don't ___

1.2.4. *To next strain*

___ you fight it 'til you tried it, do that con - ga beat.

3.

___ you fight it 'til you tried it, do the con - ga. Come ___

To Coda

(No repeat after 1st D.S.)

Verse:

1. Ev - ery - bod - y
2. It's the rhy - thm

Verse 3:
Feel the fire of desire, as you dance the night away,
'Cause tonight we're gonna party, 'til we see the break of day.

Verse 4:
Better get yourself together, and hold on to what you've got.
Once the music hits your system, there's no way you're gonna stop.

(To Chorus:)

CUTTING THE CAKE
(The Farmer in the Dell)

TRADITIONAL
Arranged by PAMELA SCHULTZ

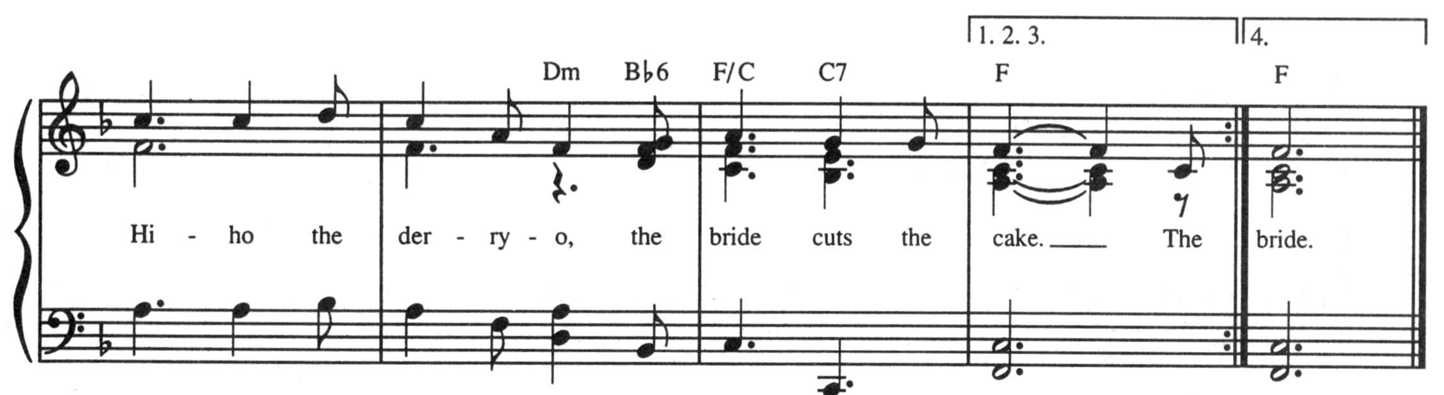

Verse 2:
The groom cuts the cake.
The groom cuts the cake.
Hi-ho the derry-o,
The groom cuts the cake.

Verse 3:
The bride feeds the groom.
The bride feeds the groom.
Hi-ho the derry-o,
The bride feeds the groom.

Verse 4:
The groom feeds the bride.
The groom feeds the bride.
Hi-ho the derry-o,
The groom feeds the bride.

ELECTRIC SLIDE

a/k/a ELECTRIC BOOGIE

Words and Music by
NEVILLE LIVINGSTON

G♭6
D♭
G♭6
lec - tric.) Rap: Dig Miss Kelly with electric belly. She's moving with electric, she sure got the boogie.
D♭
G♭6
You got - ta know__ it, (It's e - lec - tric, boog - ie woog - ie, woog - ie.) that
D♭
G♭6
you can't__ hold__ it. (It's e - lec - tric, boog - ie woog - ie, woog - ie.) But you
D♭
G♭6
D♭
To Coda
know it's there,__ here, there, and ev - 'ry - where.__

Verse:
G♭6
D♭
1. I've got to move.
2.3.4. See additional lyrics
I'm going on a party ride.
I've got to groove, groove, groove,
and from this music I just can't hide.
1.3.
2.
D.S. 𝄋
4.
D.C. al Coda
2. Are you coming
4. I've got to
2. Some

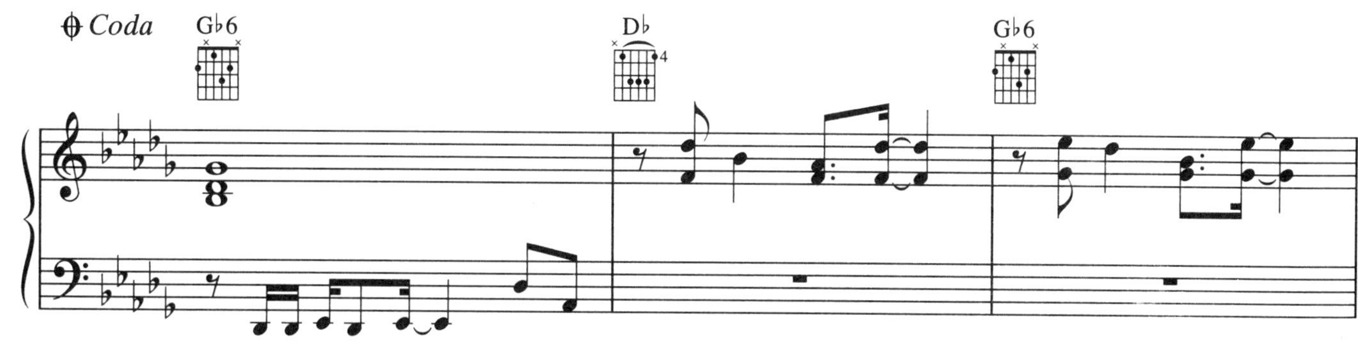

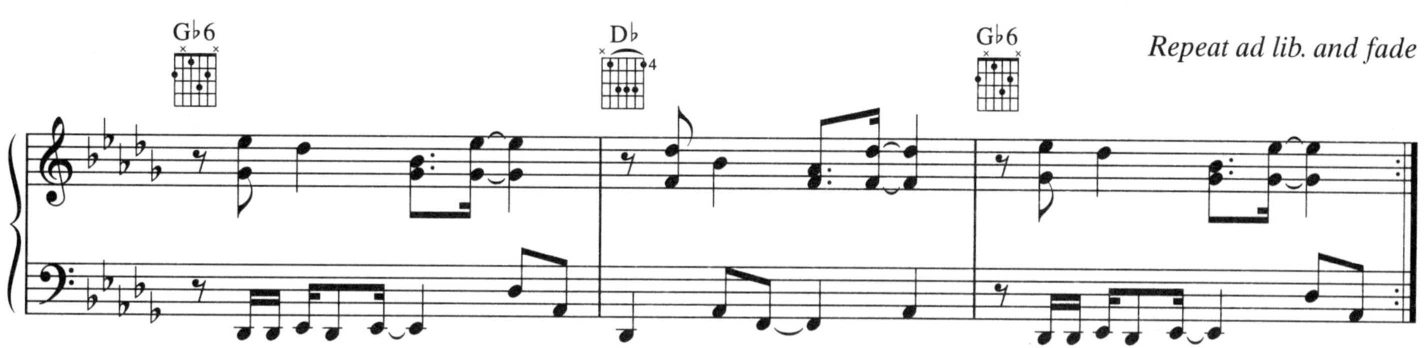

Verse 2:
Are you coming with me?
Come, let me take you on a party ride,
And I'll teach you, teach you, teach you,
I'll teach you the electric slide.

Chorus 2:
Some say it's a mystic.
It's electric, boogie woogie, woogie.
You can't resist it.
It's electric, boogie woogie, woogie.
You can't do without it.
It's electric, boogie woogie, woogie.
Rap:
Say to dig Miss Molly.
She's feeling jolly.
She's moving with electric.
She sure got to boogie.
Don't want to lose it.
It's electric, boogie woogie, woogie.
You got to use it.
It's electric, boogie woogie, woogie.
But you know it's there,
Here, there, and ev'rywhere.

Verse 3:
Instrumental

Verse 4:
I've got to move.
Come, let me take you on a party ride,
And I'll teach you, teach you, teach you,
I'll teach you the electric slide.

HOT HOT HOT

Words and Music by
ALPHONSUS CASSELL

C
Bb/C
F
Bb
Me mind on fi - re,
See peo - ple rock - in',
me soul on fi - re, feel - in'
hear peo - ple chant - in' feel - in'
hot hot_ hot.
All the peo - ple
Keep up the spir - it,
all a - round me feel - in'
come on let's do it, feel - in'
A - what to
It's in the
do
air,
on a night like
cel - e - bra - tion

C Bb/C F Bb C Bb/C
this. Is it sweet? I can't re - sist. We
time. Is it sweet? Cap- ti - vate your mind. We
F Bb C Bb/C F Bb
need a par - ty sound, a fun - da - men - tal
have this par - ty sound, this fun - da - men - tal
C Bb/C F Bb C Bb/C
charm, so we can rhum - bum - bum - bum. Yeah, ba-
charm,
F Bb C Bb/C F Bb
rhum - bum - bum - bum. Feel - in' hot hot_ hot.

C
Bb/C
F
Bb
C
Bb/C
Feel - in' hot hot_ hot.
1.
F
Bb
C
Bb/C
F
Bb
C
Bb/C
3
La la rhum - bum - bum.
2.
F
Dm
C
F
Bb
C
O-
Tacet
lé o - lé o - lé o - lé, o - lé o - lé o - lé o - lé, o-

F
B♭
B♭/C
F
B♭
lē o - lē o - lē o - lē, o - lē o - lē o -
B♭/C
F
lē o - lē.
Tacet
(Spoken:)Peo - ple in a par - ty hot hot hot.
Peo - ple in a par - ty hot hot hot. They
come to the par - ty know - in' what they got._ They
come to the par - ty know - in' what they got._
I'm hot, you're hot.
He's hot, she's hot.
I'm hot, you're hot.
He's hot, she's hot.
F
(Re - al hot,

C
F
C
re - al hot,
re - al hot.)
F
C7
F
C7
F
C7
F
C7
F
(Spoken:) How you feel - in'? Hot hot_ hot.
C7
F
C7
Repeat and fade
How you feel - in'? Hot hot_ hot.
How you feel - in'? Hot hot_ hot.
How you feel - in'? Hot hot_ hot.

MACARENA

Words and Music by
ANTONIO ROMERO
and RAFAEL RUIZ

Ab5
Gb5
Eb5
Da - le‿a tu cuer - po‿a-le-grí - a Ma-ca-re - na, eh, Ma - ca - re - na.
Da - le‿a tu cuer - po‿a-le-grí - a Ma-ca - re - na que tu cuer-po‿es pa' dar - le‿a-le-grí-a‿y co - sa bue-na.
Da - le‿a tu cuer - po‿a-le-grí - a Ma-ca - re - na, eh, Ma - ca - re - na. 1. Ma-ca -
Versos 1 y 3:
re - na tie-ne‿un no-vio que se lla-ma, que-se lla-ma de‿a-pe - lli - do Vi - to - ri - no. Y‿en la
3. See additional lyric

Ab5
Gb5
Ab5
Gb5
Eb5
ju - ra de ban-de - ra del mu-cha-cho
se la dió con dos a - mi-gos. Ma-ca -
Puente:
Db5
C5
re - na tie-ne un no-vio que se lla-ma, que se lla-ma de a-pe-lli - do Vi - to - ri - no y en la
Bb5
Eb5
Ab5
Gb5
Eb5
ju - ra de ban-de - ra del mu-cha-cho
se la dió con dos a - mi-gos.
Coro:
Ab5
Gb5
Ab5
Gb5
Da - le a tu cuer - po a-le-grí - a Ma-ca - re - na que tu cuer-po es pa' dar - le a-le-grí-a y co-sa bue-na.

Ab5
Gb5
Ab5
Gb5
Eb5
Da - le a tu cuer - po a - le - grí - a Ma - ca - re - na,
eh,
Ma - ca - re - na.
Ab5
Gb5
Ab5
Gb5
Da - le a tu cuer - po a - le - grí - a Ma - ca - re - na que tu
cuer - po es pa' dar - le a - le - grí - a y co - sa bue - na.
Ab5
Gb5
Ab5
Gb5
Eb5
Al Coda
Da - le a tu cuer - po a - le - grí - a Ma - ca - re - na,
eh,
Ma - ca - re - na.
2. Ma - ca -
Versos 2 y 4:
Ab5
Gb5
Ab5
Gb5
re - na, Ma - ca - re - na, Ma - ca - re - na,
que te
gus - tan los ve - ra - nos de Mar - be - lla.
Ma - ca -
4. See additional lyric

1.
Ab5
Gb5
Ab5
Gb5
Eb5
re - na, Ma - ca - re - na, Ma - ca - re - na, que te gus - ta la mo - vi - da gue - rri - lle - ra.
2.
D.S. 𝄋 al Coda
Ab5
Gb5
Ab5
Gb5
Eb5
ju - ra de ban - de - ra del mu - cha - cho se la dió con dos a - mi - gos. Ma - ca -
Coda
Coro:
Ab5
Gb5
Ab5
Gb5
Da - le a tu cuer - po a - le - grí - a Ma - ca - re - na que tu cuer - po es pa' dar - le a - le - grí - a y co - sa bue - na.
1.-5.
Ab5
Gb5
Ab5
Gb5
Eb5
Da - le a tu cuer - po a - le - grí - a Ma - ca - re - na, eh, Ma - ca - re - na.

Verso 3:
Macarena sueña con el Corte inglés
Y se compra los modelos mas modernos.
Le gustaría vivir en Nueva York
Y ligar un novio nuevo.

Puente 2:
Macarena sueña con el Corte inglés
Y se compra los modelos mas modernos.
Le gustaría vivir en Nueva York
Y ligar un novio nuevo.
(Al Coro:)

Verso 4:
Macarena tiene un novio que se llama,
Que se llama de apellido Vitorino.
Y en la jura de bandera del muchacho
Se la dió con dos amigos.

Puente 3:
Macarena tiene un novio que se llama,
Que se llama de apellido Vitorino.
Y en la jura de bandera del muchacho
Se la dió con dos amigos.
(Al Coro:)

REMOVING THE GARTER

(The Stripper)

Tempo di blues

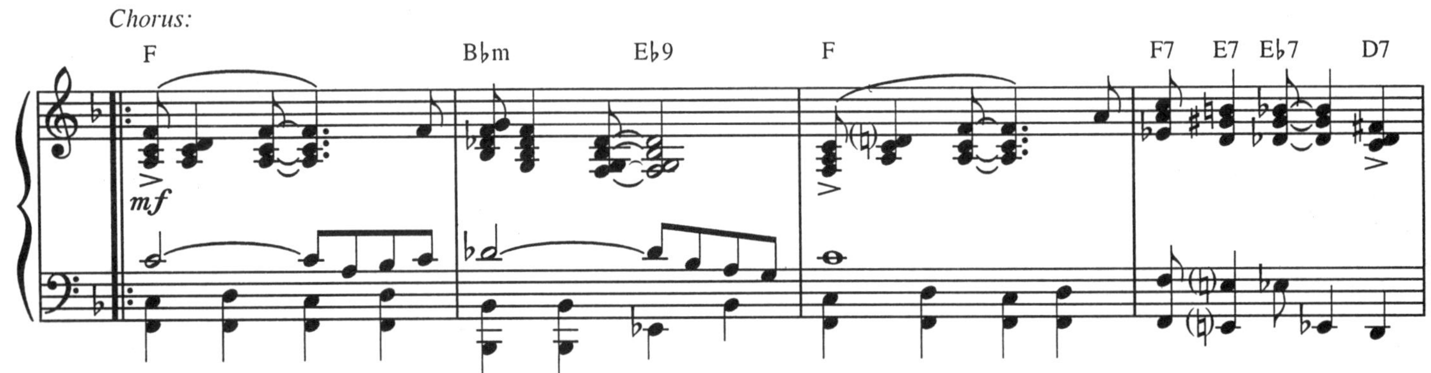

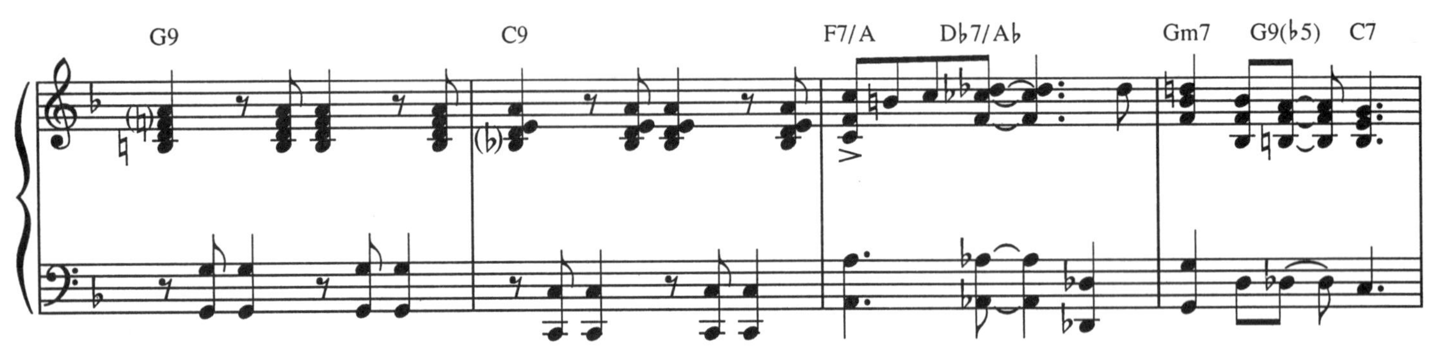

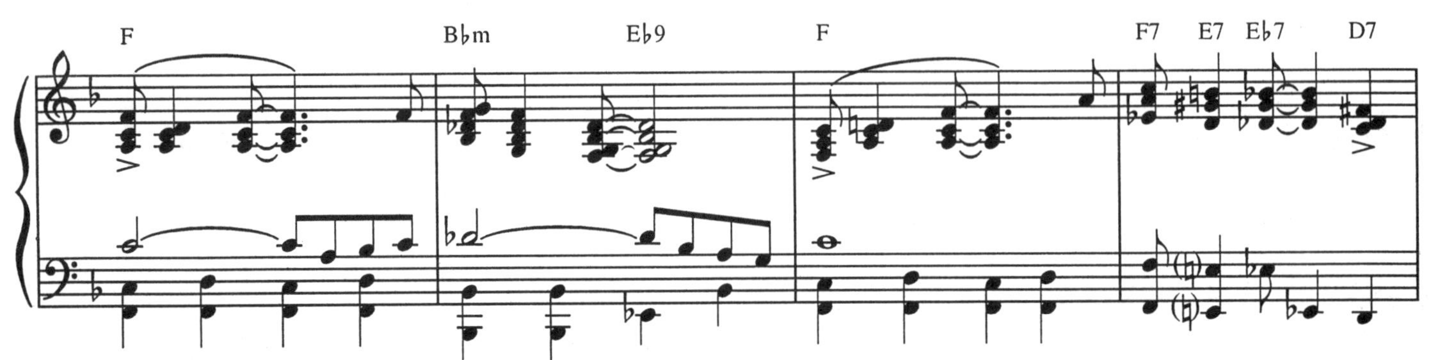

G9
C9
F
F7
Fdim
F
F7
f
F7
F7
f
8va
8va
8va
G7
C7
Gm7/C
Cdim
C7
F
B♭m
E♭9
mf
F
F7
E7
E♭7
D7
G9
C9
1.
F
A♭dim
C7
Gm7
C7
2.
F/A
D♭7/A♭
Gm7
C7(♭5)
F
f

TARANTELLA
(Italian Wedding Dance)

TRADITIONAL
Arranged by PAMELA SCHULTZ

Dm
Am
Dm6
Am
E7
1.
Am
cresc.
f
mf
2.
Am
f
Am
Dm
Am
E7
Am
E7
1.
Am
2.
Am
G7
C
G7
C
G7
1.
C
G7
2.
C

THROWING THE BOUQUET

(Take Me Out to the Ball Game)

By
JACK NORWORTH and
ALBERT VON TILZER
Arranged by PAMELA SCHULTZ

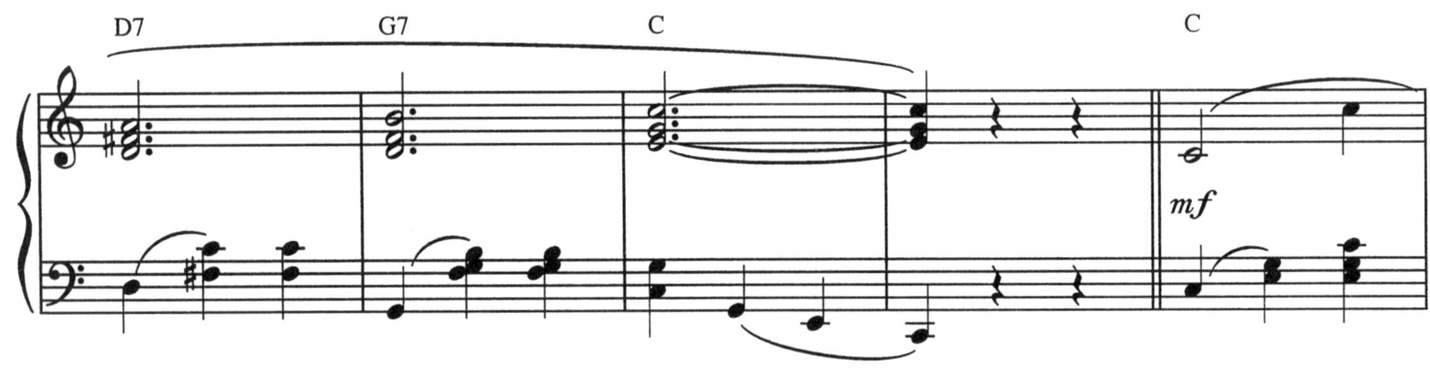

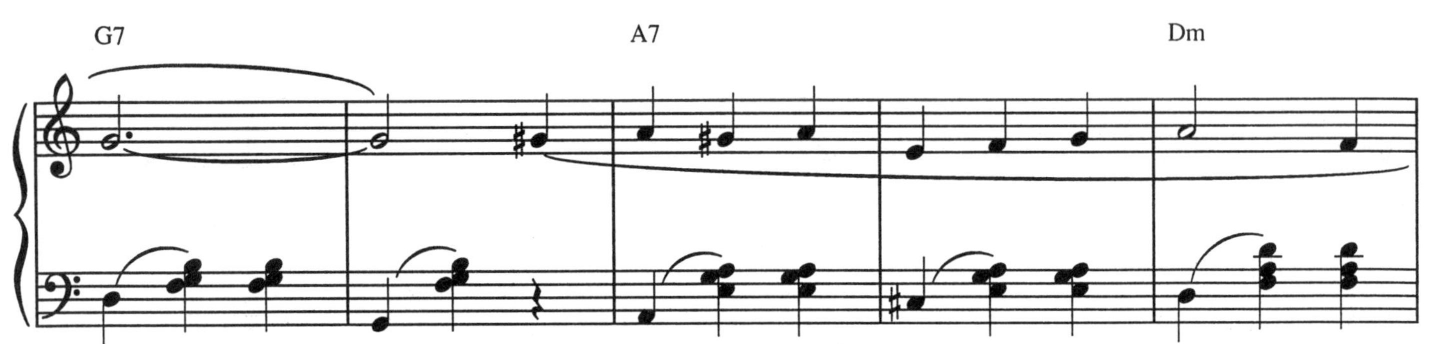

D7
G

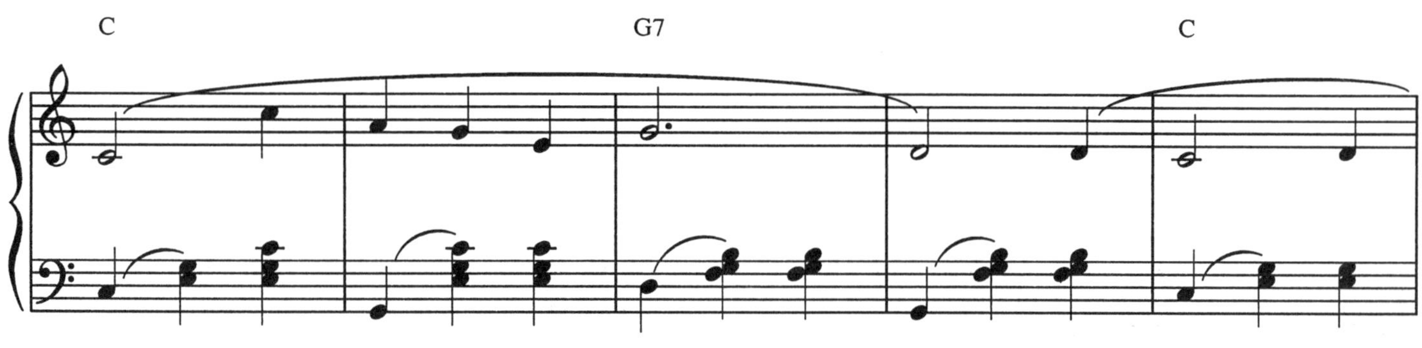
C
G7
C

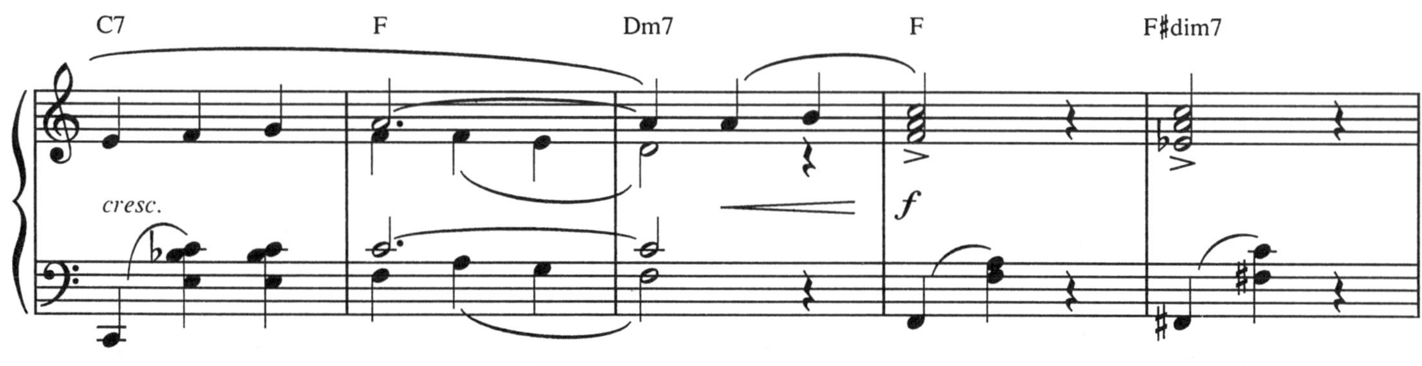
C7
F
Dm7
F
F♯dim7
cresc.
f

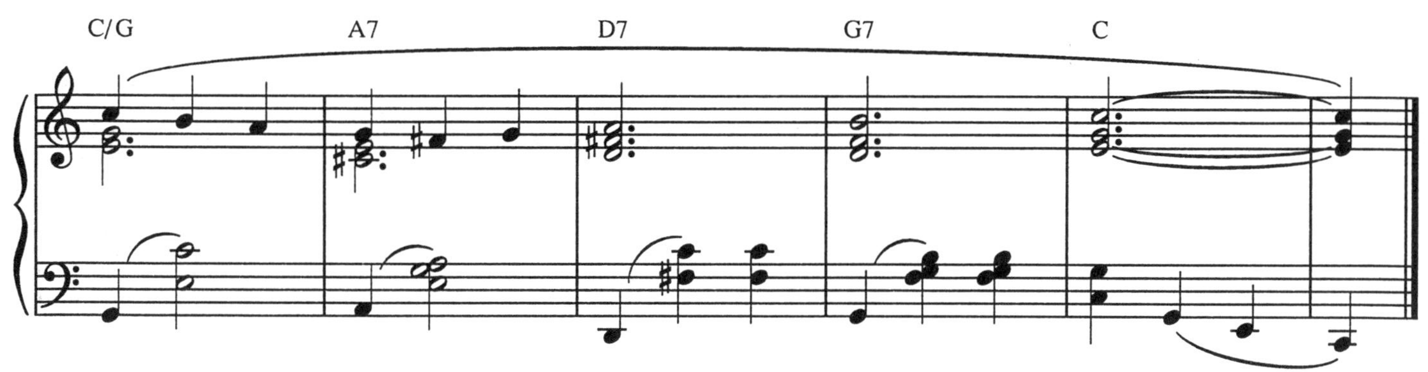
C/G
A7
D7
G7
C

MEXICAN HAT DANCE

TRADITIONAL
Arranged by PAMELA SCHULTZ

feet it is heav - en - ly
plea - sure, to be
match - ing it mea - sure for
C7
mea - sure, with my
sweet - heart, my love and my
trea - sure, while I
wait for the chance to be
F
kissed. Though my
G7
love may not have much di -
C
ne - ro, he's a
G7
hand - some and young ca - ba -
C
lle - ro, and I'll
G7
dance all a - round his som -
C
bre - ro. It's my
G7
dar - ling's big Mex - i - can

C F

hat. But its brim was not made just for danc - ing. It is

C7

al - so quite good for ro - manc - ing, for my sweet-heart is al - ways en -

F

tranc - ing in his won - der - ful Mex - i - can hat.

f

C7

1. F 2. F